101 TIPS

FOR EVANGELISM

Practical Ways to Enhance Your Witness

101 TIPS

FOR EVANGELISM

Practical Ways to Enhance Your Witness

R. LARRY MOYER

HENDRICKSON
PUBLISHERS

101 Tips for Evangelism:
Practical Ways to Enhance Your Witness

© 2017 Hendrickson Publishers Marketing, LLC
P. O. Box 3473
Peabody, Massachusetts 01961-3473
www.hendrickson.com

ISBN 978-1-61970-884-6

Printed in the United States of America

First Printing — January 2017

Library of Congress Cataloging-in-Publication Data

A catalog record for this book is available from the Library of Congress.
Hendrickson Publishers Marketing, LLC ISBN 978-1-61970-884-6

CONTENTS

RECOGNIZE THAT EVANGELISM IS GOD'S WORK

CONTENTS

PREPARE YOUR HEART TO SHARE THE GOSPEL

UNDERSTAND YOUR AUDIENCE

SPEAK THE TRUTH IN LOVE

CONCENTRATE ON BEING FAITHFUL

HELP NEW CHRISTIANS GROW

ABOUT THE AUTHOR

ABOUT EVANTELL

INTRODUCTION

There's nothing on earth I'd rather do than evangelize. God, in His gracious kindness, has allowed me to present the gospel to hundreds of thousands over the last forty-plus years.

As I have done so, under God's guidance, I've learned tips through Scripture and experience. I can sincerely say that God has used them to make me a more effective evangelist. Along the way, I've often thought, "Wow! I wish I would've learned that sooner." But God knows what He is doing and in His own time, He has enabled me to learn and grow.

I hope as I share these tips with you your love for unbelievers is enhanced and your desire to reach them increases. If that happens, this book will be worth all the time and effort. Most of all, thank you for cultivating a heart for the people who need to hear the greatest message of all: Christ died for your sins and rose from the dead.

R. Larry Moyer

GET STARTED

TIP #1

EVANGELISM ALWAYS STARTS WITH OBEDIENCE.

First Things First

Trite, isn't it? How many times have you heard the phrase used? It may refer to items for an agenda or activities for the weekend. It may be used for the five-year plan we have for our vocation or the five-day plan we have for our vacation. *First things first.*

Nowhere is that more true than the area of evangelism. Without the right starting point, we let fears and insecurities keep us from fulfilling the Great Commission (Matthew 28:19–20). How many times have you heard the following remarks in evangelism or used them yourself?

- "I wish I knew how to turn a conversation to spiritual things. That would help me so much in evangelism."

- "I'm so afraid. If I could deal with rejection, I'd evangelize more."

- "Once I learn how to answer questions and objections I know I will be more consistent in evangelism."

- "I'm going to study what the New Testament says about evangelism. I think that will increase my concern for the lost."

- "I am going to spend more time in prayer before evangelizing. I think that will help me a lot."

All of those are appropriate. Learning how to turn conversations to spiritual things is a good skill to develop.

Overcoming fear instead of letting it overcome you will make a difference in evangelism. Learning how to answer questions and objections will make you more confident in talking to the lost. Every believer is helped by knowing what the New Testament says, but that should never be a block to evangelizing. Prayer is an essential part of effective evangelism, but even prayer needs to be followed by obedience.

None of these, though, is the starting point. The starting point is obedience. After all, that is where Christ started with the disciples. In Luke 5, after a fruitless night of fishing, He said to them, "Launch out in the deep and let down your nets for a catch" (v. 4). Peter responded, "Master, we have toiled all night and caught nothing; nevertheless at Your word I will let down the net." Even though an entire night had not produced one fish, they were resolved they would do what Jesus said. After taking in a net-breaking, boat-sinking load, Christ drove his lesson home. He said, "Do not be afraid. From now on you will catch men" (v. 10). He wanted to teach them to do what he said when he said to do it no matter how crazy it seemed. Everything starts not with knowing how or training, but with obedience.

Do everything you can to learn and grow in evangelism, but be careful to put first things first—obedience.

TIP #2

THE BIBLICAL MESSAGE IS WHAT MATTERS MOST IN EVANGELISM.

What Is Your Message?

Two of my professors in seminary impacted my life by both saying the same thing. They used different words of course, but the message was the same. I've never forgotten what they said: "You always have to ask, 'If you were the devil, how would you do it?'"

Satan is having a heyday in the church. He's distracting churches from examining the message with questions about methods. Churches are asking, "How do we reach the people of today's generation?" One church uses movie theater clips to grab people's attention. Another emphasizes a quiet and reverent atmosphere of a more traditional style. Still another stresses the creative use of modern technology. While none of these approaches are wrong in themselves, our first and foremost concern is our message for unbelievers. If the message isn't right, the methods don't matter. They may be attractive in drawing people to church, but if the message isn't correct, people will not come to God.

In their good intentions to reach unbelievers, some churches try to make Christianity look attractive by presenting a wrong focus and false expectations of what it means to become a Christian. "Come to Christ. He'll change your marriage." "With Him, you can experience prosperity, not poverty." "Tired and lonely? He'll change all of that!" "Tired of being selfish? Come to Christ. He'll make you selfless."

Unfortunately, that is not the message. Paul the apostle said in 2 Corinthians 5:20, "Now then, we are ambassadors for

Christ, as though God were pleading through us: we implore you on Christ's behalf, be reconciled to God." If Christ were to walk the surface of the earth today, His message would be reconciliation. Reconciliation should then be the focus of our message, too. God has taken those who are His enemies and made it possible for us to be His friends. The message we have for the lost is that we are all sinners, Christ died as our substitute and rose again, and through personal trust in Him alone, we can enjoy His free gift of eternal life. God has compassion on all of our hurts and will eventually heal us, if not now, then when Christ returns, but loneliness or broken marriages are not *the* issue at the heart of the gospel. It is our eternal destiny.

If people don't understand that message, methods don't matter. Methods may bring people to church, but only the message brings them to God. Start with the question, "What are we telling the lost?" If the message isn't right, whatever means of communication we are using won't help.

TIP #3

WHETHER OR NOT YOU HAVE THE GIFT OF EVANGELISM IS NOT THE ISSUE.

All Responsible, Some Gifted

When confronted with an opportunity to evangelize, some believers protest, "But I don't have the gift of evangelism." Because they don't have the spiritual gift of evangelism, they push off the expectation of evangelism. They don't speak to unbelievers about Christ. Their misunderstanding of spiritual gifts in comparison to Christian responsibility becomes their excuse.

Yes, many have a particular, God-given ability in evangelism. Ephesians 4:11 says, "And He Himself gave some to be apostles, some prophets, some evangelists, and some pastors and teachers." Biblically defined, the gift of evangelism is the ability to communicate the gospel to sinners and equip the saints to do the same. It has both a reaching side (directed to non-Christians) and an equipping side (directed to Christians).

Understand, also, that the Bible speaks of evangelism as a responsibility for *all* believers. Once we trust Christ as Savior, God invites us to be His disciples and follow after Him. *Disciple* means learner. What is the first thing Jesus taught His original followers? Evangelism. In Matthew 4:19, He said, "Follow Me, and I will make you fishers of men." Evangelism is first and foremost an issue of discipleship. If, as believers, we are going to follow after Christ and learn what He has to teach us, we must in some way be involved in evangelism.

"But I don't know what to say or do," you might say. Be encouraged! The first disciples didn't either. But look carefully at Christ's words. "Follow Me and I will *make* you fishers of men" (emphasis mine). Jesus Himself promises to personally teach you everything you need to know. If you will do the following, He will do the teaching. The first disciples knew absolutely zero about introducing others to Christ, but He taught, and they learned. They were not fishers of men; they *became* fishers of men.

Though some Christians have a special ability, all have a responsibility. Don't confuse the two. If you don't have the gift, be encouraged. God can and will still use you as a disciple in one of the greatest privileges of life—introducing others to Christ. Don't allow "I don't have the gift" to hold you back. Believers who do not possess the gift of evangelism have led multitudes to Christ. If you do have the gift, think of the help you can be to those who do not have your God-given ability. Those with a gift are often a tremendous help to those without it.

TIP #4

BEING IN LOVE WITH JESUS MAKES A HUGE DIFFERENCE.

When You Love Someone

A friend of mine asked his teenage son, who was very spiritually minded, a good question. It caused the son to pause before answering. The question was, "I know you like Jesus, but are you in love with Him?"

This is a good question for all of us, especially as we think in terms of evangelism. If we genuinely love God, our foremost desire is to please Him and obey Him: "If you love Me, keep My commandments" (John 14:15).

Some may argue that there is no command in the Bible to evangelize. This is true. Evangelism is assumed more than it is asserted. The attitude inherent in Scripture seems to be, "Why *wouldn't* you tell others about Him?" Even what is commonly referred to as the Great Commission in Matthew 28:18–20 is actually a command to make disciples. Understand, though, that we must first share the good news in order to then make disciples. The second must follow the first. So evangelism is intrinsic to the Great Commission.

But back up. One of the clearest statements in the Bible that defines Christ's purpose in coming is Luke 19:10: "For the Son of Man has come to seek and to save that which was lost." To get close to the heart of Christ is to be impacted by His love for the lost. It's virtually impossible to love the Lord without loving the lost. When you love someone so many things happen, including the desire to become closer by sharing his concerns and burdens. The more we love Christ, the more burdened we will be to reach the people He loves—those who have not met Him and have no idea Who they are missing.

Loving Him even takes away the concern about how someone may respond to us. Consider a husband who is in love with his wife and vice versa. How others feel about the spouse is immaterial. A husband wants his friends to know how he feels about his wife and how grateful he is for her. After all, *she* is the one he is in love with. He insists with his friends, "You really need to meet her." When we are in love with Christ, it has the same results. They may not feel about Him the way we do, but they so need to meet Him.

All Christians like Jesus, but it should always go deeper than that. Fall in love with Him. You'll want everyone you know to meet Him.

TIP #5

DEVELOP A REPERTOIRE
OF QUESTIONS.

Helpful Questions

Anyone experienced in evangelism will tell you that questions are tremendously helpful in talking with unbelievers. They arouse attention, provoke thought, and invite interaction. But one question is not sufficient. Since you are dealing with a variety of people, you need a variety of questions.

Track your way through the gospel of John as well as the book of Acts and note the variety of questions used in introducing people to the Savior. To the Samaritan woman of John 4 who came to draw water, Christ used a very simple request, "Give Me a drink" (v. 7). In the original language that is actually a polite request—"If you would, could I have a drink?" He then took her from the water that could not satisfy to the only water that could. To the blind man already sensitized to spiritual things, Christ used a very direct question, "Do you believe in the Son of God?" (John 9:35). Similarly, what better question could Philip have asked a man already engaged in the study of the Scriptures than, "Do you understand what you are reading?" (Acts 8:30).

There are two things that characterize the questions used throughout Scripture to engage in evangelistic conversation: 1) questions that are common sense, and 2) questions that pique interest and curiosity to delve deeper.

Where do you come up with these questions? Experience. Soon a person's "basket" or repertoire is filled with effective questions. Not every question fits every situation, but one of several could be used for a particular setting.

The question, "Has anyone ever taken a Bible and shown you how you can know for sure you are going to heaven?" is effective for anyone who has indicated an interest in spiritual things. A question that can be used with a wide variety of people to delve into spiritual matters is, "If there is one question you could ask God, what would it be?" A question that generates general discussion is, "Why do you think the problems of the world seem to be getting worse instead of better?" That discussion may allow you to talk with them about the ultimate problem solver, Jesus Christ. If someone expresses a wide variety of interests but nothing spiritual, ask them, "Are you interested in spiritual things?" If you are talking with someone who refers to the passing of a loved one, a good question is, "In your opinion, what happens after death?"

Questions. Keep your basket full of them and keep adding to the basket. Who knows which question will be the next one you will find helpful?

TIP #6

YOUR PERSONALITY CAN BE A STRENGTH IN EVANGELISM.

Personality Is a Plus

You are one of a kind. The Bible says so. Psalm 139:14 says, "I will praise You, for I am fearfully and wonderfully made; marvelous are Your works, And that my soul knows very well." God carved you just the way He wanted you to be. You are His handiwork.

That includes our personalities, which, if properly used, can be a benefit in evangelism. It can help us encourage those who differ in their makeup from us.

For example, people referred to as having "choleric" personalities are often described as "take charge" people. They want to get it done. In conversations with the lost, they are not easily rattled. They easily lay aside comments or even ridicule that will hold others back. Conflict really doesn't bother them.

Unfortunately, they can sometimes have little patience with people who are fearful of evangelism or who become discouraged because of a humiliating comment made by a non-Christian. If such a person, though, can understand how he differs from others and vice versa, his personality can become an encouragement to others. Since he is not easily discouraged by conflict, he can help other believers understand how to handle ridicule and rejection.

Alternatively, those referred to as "sanguine" personalities are often described as "people" people. They are the life of the party. One I know is at her happiest meeting new people every day. She thrives on meeting people—the more the merrier. When that personality is accompanied by a heart for the lost, they find it rather easy to begin in-depth conversations that allow them to move into spiritual things and ultimately the gospel. Sometimes unbelievers are even drawn to them because they sense how much they enjoy people.

However, they can become critical of others who could sit in front of a computer all day and never talk to anyone. Intentionally or not they can criticize others for not caring about people or even for being self-absorbed. If instead they recognize the strength of their personality, they can be a big help in training others how to initiate conversations and turn them to spiritual issues. They can transfer their people skills to others.

Whatever our personalities, we should use them to help others in evangelism and encourage them where they are weak. As our personalities are a help to them, theirs can be a help to us. What better way to use our uniqueness than to help each other in our outreach to the lost?

TIP #7

WHATEVER YOUR SPIRITUAL GIFT, IT CAN BE USED TO REACH THE LOST.

Using Your Spiritual Gifts

Have you discovered your spiritual gifts and how they might be used in evangelism? The Scriptures are clear. The spiritual gift of evangelism can be used to both reach the lost and train believers in evangelism. What believers often overlook is how, *whatever* their spiritual gifts are, in some way they can be used in evangelism.

A spiritual gift is a divinely given ability to serve the body of Christ. As Ephesians 4:12–13 explains, spiritually gifted people are given to the church

> for the equipping of the saints for the work of ministry, for the edifying of the body of Christ, till we all come to the unity of the faith and of the knowledge of the Son of God, to a perfect man, to the measure of the stature of the fullness of Christ.

All believers have a spiritual gift; some have more than one. How might your spiritual gift, even though it is not the gift of evangelism, be used to serve the body of Christ and reach the lost? A careful look at several gifts will explain.

Take the gift of mercy mentioned in Romans 12:8. It could be defined as the ability to show sympathy toward the hurts of others and minister to them in their need. This can be an exceptionally special gift in evangelism. Many come to Christ in the midst of a crisis—loss of a job, loss of a mate or close friend, or sudden change in health. When one with the gift of mercy shows sympathy toward such a person and ministers to them, opportunities open up for the gospel. Believers with this gift can have a tremendous ministry to unbelievers.

Suppose one has the gift of administration mentioned in 1 Corinthians 12:28. He has a special ability to organize people toward a common goal, oversee the details that are involved, and ensure that the process runs smoothly. What better person is there to organize an outreach event or lay out the details of a church's evangelism program?

Have the gift of teaching (as seen 1 Corinthians 12:28)? God uses those believers to instruct His people in spiritual truths. Such a gifted person has the opportunity to take what the Scriptures say about evangelism and teach believers in a way that enhances their personal outreach.

Identify your spiritual gifts and then ask God, "How can I use my gifts in evangelism?" Your spiritual gifts, whatever they are, can impact the body of Christ and ultimately unbelievers.

TIP #8

YOU DON'T HAVE TO KNOW THE WHOLE BIBLE TO EVANGELIZE, JUST THE GOSPEL.

Share the Gospel, Not the Bible

Ever notice how we have a way of making many things more complicated than they need to be? It may be directions on how to get a permit to build a house or on how to return a pair of pants.

Sadly, we often do the same thing when explaining the plan of salvation. One way we complicate it is we explain the Bible, not the gospel. We seem to want to explain Genesis through Revelation to an unbeliever. They haven't even come to Christ. At this point, it's not the Bible they need; it's only the gospel.

You might say, "But the Bible is the gospel." No, the Bible *contains* the gospel. But the Bible is a whole lot more than the gospel. It contains vital information on how to raise your children, how to spend your money, how to love your enemy, how to participate in a local church, how to understand end-time events, and much more. The historical elements of the gospel are contained in 1 Corinthians 15:3–5:

> For I delivered to you first of all that which I also received: that Christ died for our sins according to the Scriptures, and that He was buried, and that He rose again the third day according to the Scriptures, and that He was seen by Cephas, then by the twelve.

Note the four verbs. Christ *died*, He was *buried* (the proof that He died), He *rose* again, and He was *seen* (the proof that

He rose). So the gospel can be reduced to ten words: "Christ died for our sins and rose from the dead." *That* is the message we have for unbelievers. That is what God calls, "the power of God to salvation for everyone who believes" (Romans 1:16).

So why not get excited about evangelism! We don't have to be a seminary student with a thorough knowledge of the Scriptures. We don't have to be an intellectual who can refute every argument or answer every question. We don't have to be a person gifted in evangelism. All we have to be is someone who explains the simple message of the gospel.

Your lost acquaintance doesn't need the sixty-six books of the Bible. He can learn those later. Right now he needs the ten words of the gospel—Christ died for our sins and rose from the dead.

TIP #9

GROWTH IN GRACE AND KNOWLEDGE WILL HELP YOUR EVANGELISM.

Both Are Needed

Sometimes the simplest things the Bible says can be the most impacting and also the most helpful in your personal outreach. In 2 Peter 3:18, Peter challenged the church saying, "But grow in the grace and knowledge of our Lord and Savior Jesus Christ." *Grow* has the idea of a never-ending process. Peter said that such growth will help protect one from error (see 2 Peter 1–2). Knowing God's Word helps you identify error when you hear it, but there are other benefits.

Peter emphasizes two realms of growth: grace and the knowledge of Christ. *Grace* means undeserved favor and deals with the entire realm in which God lives and extends His kindness toward us. God dishes out favor upon favor to those who don't deserve it. Each day He showers us with what we don't deserve, like forgiveness when we wrong Him. As we grow in grace we find ourselves responding to unbelievers the way He responds to us. Since He is long-suffering toward us, we can be long-suffering toward them, accepting injury without fighting back. We can be humble in our approach to them because He humbled Himself and died on a cross for us. We can love the unlovely because He loved us as unlovely sinners.

Knowledge doesn't just mean to know Him as Savior, but to *deepen* in that knowledge of who He is. It means to know Him so you begin to understand more about who He is and how He interacted with people during His time on earth. You increase your understanding of how He responded to those who worshiped Him and those who didn't. You learn more about His teachings concerning God, love, life, money, the here and now, the hereafter, and a host of other things.

That deepening of your knowledge, along with a deeper understanding of grace, teaches you how to respond to un-believers' actions and comments. The more you grow in grace and the knowledge of Christ, the more you feel equipped to speak to the lost. Who else better to equip you than the Master Himself? In words and action, you respond to unbelievers the way He desires that you would. In addition, your passion for the lost increases. How can you grow close to someone who loved the lost the way Christ did and not be changed?

Grace and the knowledge of Christ. Grow in them. You will be drawn closer to the lost as you do and will be better equipped to evangelize.

TIP #10

A PROPER ATTITUDE CAN MAKE YOU A WINSOME PERSON TO LISTEN TO.

Don't Downplay Attitude

Have you noticed that some people are like magnets? There is something about them that just draws you to them. There's something about them that others really like. Often it goes far beyond anything they say. It has to do with their attitude, their demeanor, the entire way they come across.

A good example is Daniel in the Bible: "Then this Daniel distinguished himself above the governors and satraps, because an excellent spirit was in him; and the king gave thought to setting him over the whole realm" (Daniel 6:3).

Daniel had a lot about him with which to be impressed. He set a high standard in the way he conducted himself. He was a capable statesman and businessman, an interpreter of dreams and a gifted prophet. Courage, self-control, and integrity marked his life. What this verse seems to be alluding to, though, is not just the commendable way he did his job, but his attitude in doing it. He was the kind of person you wanted to be around and hoped that some of him might rub off on you. So faultless was he in what he did and the attitude in which he did it that even his enemies found no basis to accuse him: "So the governors and satraps sought to find some charge against Daniel concerning the kingdom; but they could find no charge or fault, because he was faithful; nor was there any error or fault found in him" (v. 4).

You can imagine the impact this had upon some who did not know the God he knew. Admittedly his good attitude created some problems. When his enemies wanted to accuse him the only thing they could bring before King Darius was that he prayed three times a day (Daniel 6:13). But again, it was not just what Daniel did; it was his attitude that was so winsome, what the Bible calls an "excellent spirit" (v. 3). No doubt many, one of whom was the king, would have said, "There is something about that guy I really like."

Attitude matters. People notice not merely what we do, but the attitude in which it is done. A winsome attitude draws others to us and causes our message to be heard more quickly and clearly. The lack of a proper spirit can cause our message to be dismissed.

Does the "excellent spirit" that distinguished Daniel distinguish you?

TIP #11

TO BE CONSISTENT IN EVANGELISM, YOU MUST MASTER A METHOD.

A Hallmark of Those Who Share Christ

When I taught about choosing one method to use in evangelism, one man protested, "I don't have a method of presenting the gospel. I don't think I have ever presented it the same way to two people." So I asked him how he did it. Interestingly enough, he had a method. He came into it differently and out of it differently, but there *was* a basic method he used.

Anyone consistent in evangelism has a basic method. That method gives you two things: confidence and consistency. Evangelism can then become a regular occurrence instead of an exception in your life.

Check out Acts 17:2: "Then Paul, as his custom was, went in to them, and for three Sabbaths reasoned with them from the Scriptures." Whatever method he used, Paul had a way of laying out the truth of the Scripture for his audience. Had you listened to him several times, you would have probably seen similarities in how he approached his non-Christian audiences. Having a basic approach established, he could change it as necessary depending on his audience. Similarly, a good friend of mine is a heart surgeon. He has a basic method for performing bypass surgeries, but he can flex as necessary depending on the patient's need.

A method gives you a way to present the gospel that lays out something that is God-given and driven in a way people can understand it. Method gives you know-how.

But doesn't that method make you canned versus caring? Doesn't it turn you into a robot? It does just the opposite.

It allows you to be the most sensitive, caring, and attentive you've ever been toward the lost. Having a method, you can now relax, watch their expressions, and observe any nervousness in talking about spiritual things. You can watch how little or how much they smile. You can pick up on terminology they use. You can sense if they're confused because your eyes are glued on theirs. You become a tremendous listener because knowing how you are going to present the gospel lets you focus on them. Now you know how best to proceed, what to review, where to illustrate, when to advance, and when to back off. In short, a method frees you up to do the best job of caring and communicating that you have ever done. It even allows you to flex as necessary depending on the conversation or circumstances.

Want to be the most caring person you've ever been in evangelism? Master a method.

TIP #12

"LESS IS MORE" WHEN IT COMES TO SHARING SCRIPTURE WITH UNBELIEVERS.

A Few Are Better Than Many

Ever receive a Christmas gift that was one those "put it together yourself" items? You looked at all the parts and it became very intimidating. You breathed a sigh of relief when you found the manual that outlined the whole process in several easy to follow steps.

The Bible in its entirety can be an overwhelming book, especially to unbelievers, so we must be selective when presenting the gospel. If several verses explain what we want them to know, it's better not to use several dozen. Showing them too many verses may overwhelm them.

Ask yourself, "What do I really want the lost to understand?" It is the three parts of the salvation message—that we are sinners, Christ died for us and arose, and we have to trust Christ alone to save us.

Which verses in the Bible explain the fact that we are all sinners deserving eternal separation from God? Romans 3:23 tells us, "For all have sinned and fall short of the glory of God." Romans 6:23 tells us, "For the wages of sin is death." There are also others though. David speaks of being a sinner from birth (Psalm 51:5). Solomon made the declaration that there is no one without sin on the face of the earth (Ecclesiastes 7:20). Each one of these makes the same point though. Choose the one or two that you feel would resonate best with the unbeliever.

When one thinks of Christ's substitutionary death that paid for our sins, John 3:16 naturally comes to mind. Romans 5:8 also expresses it clearly: "But God demonstrates His own love toward us, in that while we were still sinners, Christ died for us." Other verses that speak of His sin payment for our sin debt include Isaiah 53:6 and 2 Corinthians 5:21. One or two of those will make the point.

When one thinks of the need to respond in faith, few verses say it better than Ephesians 2:8–9. "For by grace you have been saved through faith, and that not of yourselves; it is the gift of God, not of works, lest anyone should boast." One could also go to a verse such as Romans 4:5. Or go back to a verse such as John 3:16 where we are called upon to believe, to trust in Christ alone to save us.

Don't overwhelm a non-Christian with many verses when a few will suffice. When it comes to our salvation, God speaks so clearly that a few verses say it all.

TIP #13

BE CREATIVE WITH YOUR METHODS, NOT YOUR MESSAGE.

Creativity Helps

Creativity is great. It causes people to come up with ideas they never considered before. But creativity misapplied can also be dangerous. Would you enjoy being on an airplane with a pilot who came up with a new, creative way to make a landing? Would you enjoy being with a doctor who comes up with a creative combination of medicines to solve your pain problem even though it is untried and unproven? Hardly so.

Being creative can be helpful in evangelism and should even be encouraged, but make sure you're creative about the right thing. Creativity about the right thing is honoring to God and helpful to the lost. Creativity about the wrong thing is dishonoring to God and damaging to the lost.

Creativity cannot be applied to the message we have for the lost. That message never changes. Paul defined the gospel in 1 Corinthians 15:3–5, and we can summarize it in ten words, "Christ died for our sins and rose from the dead." We come to God as sinners, recognize Christ died on a cross in our place and rose again, and place our trust in Christ alone to save us. To alter that message not only gives unbelievers the wrong message, but it also invites the discipline of God. God said in Galatians 1:8, "But even if we, or an angel from heaven, preach any other gospel to you than what we have preached to you, let him be accursed."

On the other hand, creativity in our method should be welcomed and can be rewarding. What God used to reach one person is not necessarily what He will use to reach another.

Some in the New Testament came to Christ through the proclamation of the gospel to the masses (see Acts 2:14–41). Others came to Christ through a one-on-one presentation of the gospel (see Acts 8:26–39).

The methods can be as diverse as those to be reached and those who reach them. Some may respond to the printed page because they love to read. Others who are visual and enjoy what they see may be greatly impacted by a live testimony, a DVD or a TV show that teaches eternal values. Likewise, with those evangelizing, one believer might feel very comfortable with street evangelism or cold-turkey conversations. Others find such an approach difficult. Instead, they love to invite people into the comfort of their homes and talk about spiritual things.

Creativity! Go for it. Use it. But make sure you use it for your method, not the content of your message.

TIP #14

DEVELOPING YOUR MIND'S ABILITY TO THINK AND LEARN ENHANCES YOUR EVANGELISM.

Love Him with Your Mind

When Jesus told us to love Him, how did He tell us to do it? Matthew 22:37 says, "Jesus said to him, 'You shall love the Lord your God with all your heart, with all your soul, and with all your *mind*'"(emphasis mine). Note that He included the mind.

Why would I emphasize that? Although not meaning to do so, Christians sometimes advocate that the use of our intellect takes away our dependence on the Holy Spirit. In doing so, we communicate that when God forgives your sins, He also removes your brains. This is untrue.

Yes, the Bible does speak of one's intelligence keeping him from seeing the simplicity of the gospel (1 Corinthians 1:18–31). The Bible also warns about solely depending on our ability to express things intellectually to bring people to Christ (1 Corinthians 2:1–5). But neither of those passages denies the fact that God wants us to use our intelligence, discernment, and common sense.

How can we love Him with our minds in evangelism? We can be creative in how we reach out to the lost with the message of grace. Bring together the minds of innovative people and ask, "What are the possibilities in terms of how we get the message outside the walls of our church?" People who love Christ with their minds come up with great ideas.

Another way is actively engaging in conversations with unbelievers, whether we turn a conversation to spiritual things or we answer objections non-Christians have to the gospel.

The ability to think and use common sense is indispensable. God, through His Holy Spirit, brings ideas to our minds that are most effective in reaching the lost.

God gave us our minds to help us to learn and grow, including developing our skills in evangelism. One way to love Him with our minds in reaching the lost is to study and learn how to evangelize. Those effective in evangelism are eager to learn, recognizing God will do His part in developing their skills, but they also have to do theirs. They relish training in evangelism and want to develop the know-how in responding to comments made by non-Christians.

When you come to Christ, God doesn't eliminate your mind. He empowers it through the Holy Spirit to be the best it can be. So love Him with your mind. You will be encouraged with how it has enhanced your evangelism.

TIP #15

THE FACT THAT HE DIED IN OUR PLACE IS THE ESSENCE OF THE GOSPEL.

Two Words That Make a Difference

Ask the average person, "What do you have to do to gain eternal life?" The prominent answer you will receive is, "You have to be good." Why do they fail to see that eternal life is a free gift that is not deserved and cannot be earned?

It's sometimes because they miss two words in one of the clearest statements the Bible makes. Romans 5:8 says, "But God demonstrates His own love toward us, in that while we were still sinners, Christ died for us." So many people miss those two words, "for us." His death shows us how to live sacrificially and how to die to self so we can put others first, but His death was first and foremost *for us.* That means in our place. Had He not died, we would have. He was our substitute. The nails that should have been driven through our hands and feet were driven through His.

Why do those two words "for us" make such a big difference? First, the payment for sin is death. A holy God has to punish sin. That "someone" who takes our place has to be someone perfect. One sinner cannot pay for the sins of another sinner any more than one criminal can pay for another criminal's crime. The fact that God accepted His Son's death as our substitute means Jesus was who He declared Himself to be, the perfect Son of God. Had He not been, His death would never have sufficed in paying for our sins.

Second, that is why no one can even think of some way to pay for their own sin. The payment for sin has already been made. On the cross, Christ said, "It is finished!" (John 19:30).

God was completely satisfied with what His Son did in paying the price for any and all sin of any and all people. There is no way to pay for what has already been paid.

Now one can understand why no amount of goodness or good deeds can earn anyone a right relationship with God. One has to be satisfied with what satisfies God. Had He been satisfied with any goodness or good deeds on our part, His Son would not have had to die in our place.

The cross is first and foremost about substitution, not simply about sacrifice. He did not die to impress you; He died to pardon you. When you explain the gospel, be certain that unbelievers hear you—He died *for us*.

TIP #16

CONTACTS LEAD TO CONVERSATIONS, AND CONVERSATIONS LEAD TO CONVERSIONS.

The Three Cs of Evangelism

Evangelism has three Cs. *Contacts* lead to *conversations*, which lead to *conversions*. Remembering that simple principle will not only enhance your evangelism, but it will also encourage you not to make evangelism more difficult than it needs to be.

It starts with contacts. It is impossible to have personal evangelism without personal contacts. Hence you need to be what Christ was—a friend to sinners. What greater thing could be said of us than what was said of Christ? "This Man receives sinners and eats with them" (Luke 15:2). Christ's enemies meant it as a criticism, but Christ took it as a compliment. Examine everything you do at work and play. Then ask yourself, "Where on a weekly basis do I have contact with non-Christians?" It is important to have friendships with people who know the Lord, but it is equally important to have friendships with those who need the Lord.

Contact leads to conversations just like it did with Christ and the Samaritan woman of John 4. That conversation began with Christ's simple request, "Give Me a drink" (v. 7). Conversations are helpful, not so much because *you* talk, but because *they* talk. If it is your first encounter, they may share where they work or have worked, where they are from, if they are married or have children. The more you interact, the more details you learn about their lives past and present. Sometimes they go as far as to reveal their failures and successes, the highs and the lows of marriage, raising children, or work.

As they talk, you find areas where you can relate to them, similarities in background, family, and job. Secular issues allow you to go to spiritual issues such as God, prayer, religion, church, etc. Even a simple, "I'll pray for you" might invoke the response, "I could use that." This could allow you to turn the conversation to spiritual things and ultimately the gospel.

Conversations often lead to conversions, like the Ethiopian eunuch of Acts 8 who responded to Philip by saying, "I believe that Jesus Christ is the Son of God" (v. 37). The more conversations you have with non-Christians the more conversions you are likely to see. Extended conversations don't always end up with the person trusting Christ, but some do. Those that don't may plant a seed, which leads to conversions after another shares the gospel further down the path of that life.

The three Cs of evangelism—easy to remember, productive to use. *Contacts* lead to *conversations*, which lead to *conversions*.

TIP #17

PHYSICAL FITNESS CAN AFFECT YOUR EVANGELISM MORE THAN YOU THINK.

Keep in Shape Physically

No question—spiritual fitness impacts your evangelism. The closer you are to Christ the closer you will want to be to lost people. He specifically said, "for the Son of Man has come to seek and to save that which was lost" (Luke 19:10). Being close to His heart is to share His concern for the lost.

What is often overlooked, though, is how your *physical* fitness can also impact your evangelism. In no way is that to say that those with any kind of physical difficulty or handicap cannot be used in evangelism. Nothing is further from the truth. It is simply to say that along with watching how we are doing spiritually, to the best of our ability we should also guard how we are doing physically.

Interestingly enough, Paul connected physical fitness with ministry effectiveness and even future reward in 1 Corinthians 9:24–27. There he said,

> Do you not know that those who run in a race all run, but one receives the prize? Run in such a way that you may obtain it. And everyone who competes for the prize is temperate in all things. Now they do it to obtain a perishable crown, but we for an imperishable crown. Therefore I run thus: not with uncertainty. Thus I fight: not as one who beats the air. But I *discipline my body* and bring it into subjection, lest, when I have preached to others, I myself should become disqualified. (emphasis mine)

Paul used a metaphor for the spiritual life to also address the physical. He did not want a lack of self-discipline in the physical realm to cause him loss of reward when he saw the Savior face-to-face. Physical fitness matters!

Why and how is physical fitness important to evangelism? Two ways:

First, in evangelism, you are on the front lines. You are making a direct attack against Satan's kingdom (Ephesians 6:12). Spiritual battles can take a toll on us physically in terms of weariness and taxing our strength.

The second is length of life. God determines the length of our days (Job 14:5), but humanly speaking, taking care of our physical bodies can affect longevity. The more years we have, the more people we can introduce to the Savior.

God gives us many things with which we can serve Him in evangelism. One is our body. Our physical health and fitness are not totally within our control. But as much as possible, we should discipline our bodies so that they might be effective tools in evangelism.

TIP #18

SAYING A PRAYER
DOES NOT SAVE.

Be Careful Not to Mislead

Well-meaning people can sometimes do the wrong thing for the right reason. They care deeply, but sometimes do not realize how damaging or misleading words can be. As we lead people to Christ, we often bring them to a point of prayer, a time when they can verbalize to Christ their belief in Him. Sometimes, though, good intentions truncate the gospel message into praying the "sinner's prayer." "If you want to be saved, just say the sinner's prayer," one may say to the lost.

The problem is twofold. First, the "sinner's prayer" is not found in the Scriptures. One searches the Bible in vain for what is called the "sinner's prayer." Second, the unbeliever often understands that by saying a prayer one receives eternal life. Nothing could be farther from the truth. The Scriptures are clear that one is saved by trusting Christ, not by saying a prayer. One of the simplest statements of the Bible is John 6:47: "Most assuredly, I say to you, he who believes in Me has everlasting life." The moment one places his trust in Christ alone to save him, he is forever a child of God. Saying a prayer no more saves than does baptism, living a good life, going to church, keeping the commandments, or taking the sacraments.

Is the saying of a prayer at the moment of salvation helpful? Most certainly. Verbalizing to God what I am doing cements in my own mind what I have done and even begins me on a path of talking to God on a regular basis. Also, verbalizing it to God helps me in verbalizing it to others. But it is essential to understand that the utterance of a prayer does not secure our salvation. Many are saved before they say such a prayer. They've transferred their trust from whatever they trusted before to save them (their good life, church attendance, etc.) and instead now trust Christ alone to save them. At that second, they are justified before God.

We should encourage people to come to God as sinners, recognize Christ died for us and rose again, and trust Christ alone to save us. It's helpful to lead them in prayer as they tell God what they are doing and to encourage the new believer in the practice of talking to God. Be careful to explain that it is trusting Christ that saves, not saying a prayer.

TIP #19

UNBELIEVERS MUST UNDERSTAND THAT WHEN GOD SAYS ETERNAL LIFE IS FREE, HE MEANS FREE.

No Strings Attached

"Free offer, details inside." When I see those words printed on an envelope in the mail, I don't even take the time to open it. I've never received one without strings attached, something like:

- "Call this number to receive your free gift." The number you called let you know that the "free gift" was really not free.

- "Come see us and bring this card with you." Once there you learn that you must sit through a high-pressure two-hour sales presentation before getting the gift.

- "To find out if you qualify, answer these four questions and then give us a call." Interestingly enough, what was free was only free to qualified people.

I believe these popular tactics make it difficult for many people to receive God's free gift of eternal life. He says, "For the wages of sin is death, but the gift of God is eternal life in Christ Jesus our Lord" (Romans 6:23). Many respond, "There must be some kind of string attached." There isn't. When Jesus Christ paid for our sins on a cross, He paid the debt in full. That is why He declared, "It is finished!" (John 19:30). Nothing you could do could help pay for what is already paid. They may respond, "That sounds too good to be true." But just because it sounds that way, doesn't mean it isn't true.

Some Christians worry, "But, if we really stress how free it is, wouldn't that encourage someone to come to Christ and then go out and paint the town red?"

First, if that thought has *not* crossed your mind, you may not have fully grasped how free the gift is. After all, that thought crossed Paul's mind. He said in Romans 6:1, "What shall we say then, shall we continue in sin that grace may abound?"

Second, the complete freeness of that gift is the *motivation* to godly living, not sinful. Paul answered his own question by continuing, "Certainly not! How shall we who died to sin live any longer in it?" (v. 2). In fact, those Christians who don't live in gratitude for the gift find themselves more miserable than they were before they came to Christ. Their new life combined with their old sinful practices present a "conscience clash" of the worst kind.

As you evangelize be quick to explain that when others say free, they may not mean it, but God always does. The more we contemplate how completely free it is and explain that to new believers, the more motivational it becomes.

TIP #20

ALWAYS GO BACK TO THE UNDENIABLE FACT OF CHRIST'S RESURRECTION.

Facts Don't Change

A friend of mine said, "I've had moments when I've been bored with Christianity, but I've never doubted the truth of it. The facts are there."

To what facts was he referring? As he kept talking he alluded to one of the most attested facts of history: the empty tomb. Not one person has ever been able to explain it away. Of those I know who have studied the resurrection objectively, all have become Christians as result of what God revealed in that time of study. Many who have spent years in evangelism have observed the same thing. Josh McDowell testifies to the role that the study of the resurrection played in his own conversion in his book, *The Resurrection Factor*. He says, "Surprisingly, I couldn't refute Christianity because I couldn't explain away one crucial event in history—the resurrection of Jesus Christ" (8).

What does that mean in evangelism? First, always go back to the facts. The one who doubts the truth of Christianity has to explain away the empty tomb. The issue is not the trustworthiness of the Bible even though it is indeed the Word of God without error or mistake. But Christianity does not stand or fall on the Bible. It stands or falls on the resurrection. One who lays aside the Bible still has to deal with the empty tomb. Examine historical writers who refer to events surrounding the tomb of Christ. Some—even though they are not believers—will reference the resurrection as one of the most proven facts of history.

Second, our resurrection is as certain as His. Jesus answered, "A little while longer and the world will see Me no more, but you will see Me. Because I live, you will live also" (John 14:19). Anyone who has such power over the grave that He can lay His own life down and take it up again (John 10:18) can give others eternal life as well. Our faith is based on facts, not feelings. The facts have reason behind them and have never been disproved.

As we take people back to the empty tomb, we should do it with excitement. We are part of one of the most attested facts of history. His resurrection assures us of ours. He overcame the grave, and we share in the victory. What a privilege to tell the lost, "Trust Christ and your resurrection is as certain as His."

Facts don't change. His resurrection guaranteed ours and the resurrection of all who trust in Him. Announce it! Declare it! Shout it!

TIP #21

YOU DON'T HAVE TO KNOW WHAT A CULT MEMBER BELIEVES.

Know What You Believe

Believers feel pressured to understand the ins and outs of what a cultist believes in order to reach the cult member. They then study the facts and doctrines about the cult and end up discussing aspects of the cult that even the cultist doesn't understand or care about.

What is the fallacy of that approach? For one, how do you keep up? So many new cults spring up every year that it is impossible to learn and remember the facts about each one. Second, there can be two versions of the same cult, each believing something different.

But there is another fallacy. Most people in a cult are not there because of what the cult believes. Often they have little or no idea about what the core beliefs are. Most of the time, they are there because someone gave them a sense of belonging. A friend cared for them and told them, "You are one of us."

First Peter 3:15 encourages us here. Peter wrote, "But sanctify the Lord God in your hearts, and always be ready to give a defense to everyone who asks you a reason for the hope that is in you, with meekness and fear."

Peter isn't saying that one must be able to defend the Christian faith against all other philosophies and beliefs in order to evangelize. God is not expecting you to be a know-it-all or a defend-it-all in evangelism. The context is that people harm evildoers not doers of good (v. 13). But if one does suffer for doing right, Peter exhorts us not to be intimidated. Let a proper fear of God drive out your fear of man. Then when people ask why you're not afraid, you can give them "a reason for the hope that is in you, with meekness and fear," meaning you can explain the hope that is within you with reverence for God and respect for man.

You need to know what *you* believe, not what *they* believe. When they explain what they know about their cult's beliefs, you can lay it alongside of what you know to be the truth. Then you can also advise them that if they trust Christ, they will be part of an eternal family that is going to live forever in the presence of the King.

When talking to a cultist, remember, you are most likely not speaking to someone who was originally searching for truth. He was searching for a friend. Be the best friend you can be to them by letting him know what you believe and why.

RECOGNIZE THAT EVANGELISM IS GOD'S WORK

TIP #22

THE SOVEREIGNTY OF GOD PROPERLY UNDERSTOOD SHOULD COMFORT YOU IN EVANGELISM.

Do You Want in on the Action?

The sovereignty of God properly understood is always meant to be an explanation; it is never to be an excuse.

Christians discuss and even argue about issues like free will of man, predestination, election, and how they relate to salvation. In evaluating God's sovereignty versus man's will in regards to salvation, they sometimes miss the bigger picture.

The Scriptures are clear; God is sovereign. Paul testifies in Romans 9:18, "Therefore He has mercy on whom He wills, and whom He wills He hardens." Paul recognized that behind everything God does or allows there is a sovereign purpose. That brings comfort in evangelism because it means that ultimately God is in control. Nowhere in Scripture are we ever told that if an unbeliever does not come to Christ we are held responsible. God is in control, not us.

But some Christians use that understanding as an excuse. "There is no need for us to evangelize," they think. "God will save who He will."

God can and will save whom He wills, but however one understands predestination and free will is not the issue. On this side of heaven, it is doubtful that we will ever fully understand those concepts. The issue we have to face is, do we want in on the action as He brings person after person to Christ?

God's sovereignty not only relates to the outcome of evangelism, but also to the means. He has decided to use people to reach people. Being sovereign, He could have chosen any way He wanted to get the word out. He could have used a billboard or sent an angel to tell others. Instead He decided to let us do it. The people reached may be through a proclamation to the masses such as in Acts 2 or a one-on-one presentation as Philip with the Ethiopian in Acts 8. But in story after story throughout Scripture and church history, across ages and across the globe, God has used people to reach people.

If we choose not to share our faith, a sovereign God can use another believer to bring a particular unbeliever to Himself. But we miss out on the privilege and the blessing of participating in the Great Commission.

God in His sovereignty will save lost people. God in His sovereignty decided to let you in on the action. Don't decline the invitation that should be readily and excitedly accepted.

TIP #23

CONSISTENTLY ASK GOD FOR OPPORTUNITIES TO SHARE THE GOSPEL.

Have You Asked?

Ever notice how some believers have so many opportunities and others have so few? One reason could be something easily overlooked. Those who have numerous opportunities ask God for them.

Paul the apostle spoke of "doors" for the gospel, some closed and some open. It also appears that some doors were opened because he asked God to open them and even asked others to pray on his behalf for the same. In the most vivid example, he sits in prison and writes a letter to the Colossians. He did not want his physical limitations to limit him spiritually. He asked for prayer: "meanwhile praying also for us, that God would open to us a door for the word, to speak the mystery of Christ, for which I am also in chains, that I may make it manifest, as I ought to speak" (Colossians 4:3–4).

Imagine such a prayer from one who sits in prison, most likely handcuffed to a Roman soldier twenty-four hours a day. Even there, he wanted an opportunity to tell someone that Christ's death on the cross was the only means for a right standing with God. Paul's fervency to spread the gospel reveals that this kind of prayer must have been a pattern, not an exception in his life.

Now think of your schedule, the next day or the next week. Wherever you go, God can open doors. That may be as you sit in a taxi and converse with the driver who appears rather bored with his life. It may be on a flight as you talk with the person who you sense is falling apart on the inside though he appears to have everything together on the outside. The open door may be with a relative who is confronted with her own mortality when her best friend is diagnosed with cancer. The open door might be with a business acquaintance whose mate has asked for a divorce, or it may be with a neighbor whose son is getting into extensive trouble with the law.

The point is, ask God for those doors, and then get ready. Our God who hears the prayers of His children and loves the lost will answer those prayers. The answer may come more quickly than you ever thought it would. Open doors may come in some of the most unexpected ways.

Sometimes, we do not have because we have not asked. Numerous "asks" may open up numerous doors.

TIP #24

UNDERSTANDING AND VIEWING GOD AS A PERSON, NOT A THEOLOGY, MAKES A DIFFERENCE.

More Than a Set of Facts

I sometimes become alarmed at how Christians talk about God. It's almost as though He is simply a set of facts to them. I wonder if that's why non-Christians view Him as this cold figure who stands there with His arms folded as people suffer.

The study of God is called theology. Particular facts are presented about Him that prove Him to be the person He says He is. These are all good and helpful, but we must remember those facts surround a person. The warmth and caring nature of that person is seen in Jesus Christ. The Bible speaks of Him weeping at the passing of a loved one (John 11:35), becoming weary from traveling (John 4:6), and growing angry at the improper use of the temple (Matthew 21:12–13). Facts are important in increasing your knowledge of God, but it is the person of God who impacts your salvation. Coming to know Him is not coming to believe a set of facts, but embracing a person—one who is present all day, every day.

What does that mean in evangelism? Everything! It affects the description of God we present to the lost and the person we see walking by our side as we evangelize.

We present to non-Christians a God who wants to be intimately involved in their lives. His love for them is revealed in how He laid down His life in their place. Jesus Himself said, "Greater love has no one than this, than to lay down one's life for his friends" (John 15:13). Facts did not die on a cross. It was a person who felt the pain from nails driven through His hands and feet just as you or I would, but He did it so that we could be forgiven. He took the punishment we deserved. If we refuse His free offer of eternal life, He is grieved.

It also impacts how we view His involvement as we evangelize. A set of facts is aloof. People are involved with us. That means every step we take in and around unbelievers, He is there. If we are afraid to speak, He will give us the words to say. If we are uncertain how to respond to particular objections, He'll teach us. He's there every moment, every conversation.

So relax and enjoy evangelizing. The greatest person you could ever present to the lost is there. The greatest person who could ever walk alongside of you is there. Far more than a set of facts, He is a person filled with feelings for the lost and for you.

TIP #25

SINCE HE IS GOD, HE DOES NOT ALWAYS FIT A PARTICULAR PATTERN.

Expect the Unexpected

We all know what we expect God to do. But sometimes we need to expect the unexpected. After all, He is God.

John 4:35–38 is a prime example. In a few sentences, the verses wrap up Christ's ministry in Samaria:

> "Do you not say, 'There are still four months and then comes the harvest'? Behold, I say to you, lift up your eyes and look at the fields, for they are already white for harvest! And he who reaps receives rages, and gathers fruit for eternal life, that both he who sows and he who reaps may rejoice together. For in this is the saying true: 'One sows and another reaps.' I sent you to reap that for which you have not labored; others have labored, and you have entered into their labors."

Christ was only in Samaria two days, yet He did no miracles. John told us in the end of his book that Christ performed miracles to prove He was God (John 20:30–31). So why didn't He do that in Samaria?

He didn't need to! Christ used a farming analogy to explain the seasons of ministry. Just as farmers plant in one season and reap in another, so it is in ministry. The disciples expected a ministry season of sowing, but the ministry fields of Samaria were already "white for harvest." Some feel that the reason Samaria was so ripe was due to the ministry of John the Baptist or even the Old Testament prophets. Either way, the disciples were about to witness the unexpected—a field so white for harvest that when one person came to Him, many others did as well. The Scriptures explain, "And many more believed because His own word" (John 4:41).

God doesn't always fit the pattern you expect. You may not know how He has been working before you came on the scene.

You may meet someone who is far more open to the gospel than you ever imagined he would be, even though no one has ever approached him about the gospel. You may meet a person who asks you about spiritual things before you ever ask her. A relative who has always shunned you, afraid you might ask hard questions, may ask if you can do lunch.

Don't lock God in. Being God, He does the unexpected. You can't always chart what He's going to do or how He's going to work.

TIP #26

GOD USES CREATION TO SHOUT HIS PRESENCE.

The Evidence He's Real

If someone wants to hear from God directly to know He exists, they don't have far to go. They may need you to point out the obvious. Sometimes God doesn't whisper; He shouts!

Watch a deer run across the meadow. Observe a squirrel as it scampers up a tree. Study the configuration of the leaf that's fallen to the ground. Look through a telescope at a star. Climb the mountain to its peak. Let the ocean toss you about. These moments are not like some bumper stickers, easily passed over and difficult to read. They are like giant billboards shouting the same thing. The voice behind them is the Creator God, and He is not simply saying, but shouting, "I am here! I am God!"

Romans 1:20 teaches, "For since the creation of the world His invisible attributes are clearly seen, being understood by the things that are made, even His eternal power and Godhead, so that they are without excuse." A first reading of that verse shows that creation announces that there's a God. Actually the verse says much more. Creation says there is a God *of whom there is no equal*. Note the words, "His eternal power and Godhead."

One cannot look at creation and say, "There is a God" and then point to a carved image and say, "Here He is. I made Him." Instead one in awe has to say, "There is a God. He made *me*."

That is why all are without excuse. His fingerprints are *everywhere*. There is no place on earth that does not shout His presence. If one does not see God in creation, it's not because God's not visible, but instead because the person is not looking.

But will a leaf, a tree, a mountain, or a cloud explain the way of salvation to a lost person? No. The emphasis of Scripture is that if one acknowledges His presence in creation and seeks after Him, God in some way will see to it that he hears the message of the gospel. Hebrews 11:6 tells us, "He is a rewarder of those who diligently seek Him." Cornelius of Acts 10 is a good example. Convinced of God's presence he sought after Him, and God in turn caused him to hear the gospel through Peter.

As we converse with unbelievers we can remind them that God doesn't whisper His presence; He shouts it! Creation is a voice that cannot be silenced.

TIP #27

SOME APPOINTMENTS ARE DIVINELY ARRANGED TO GIVE YOU AN OPPORTUNITY FOR THE GOSPEL.

It May Not Be Just Another Meeting

We all have calendars. They may be something physical we carry with us in a pocket or purse, something digital as a smartphone application, an item maintained by an executive assistant, or something we store in the memory section of our brain. But we all have calendars where appointments are made. Sometimes we may overlook how God-driven some of those appointments may be. A human instrument, whether you or someone else, may have put the appointment on your calendar. But behind the human instrument may have been the hand of God.

In the book of Esther, Mordecai asked the queen a most piercing question. The wicked Haman had masterminded a plot to destroy all the Jews within King Ahasuerus's kingdom. Little did King Ahasuerus know that his own queen was of Jewish heritage. When Mordecai, who raised Esther, heard of the plot, he was confident that God could use anyone He wanted to save the Jewish people. He was also very confident in the sovereignty and power of God. But he recognized that the reason Esther was in the king's favor might have been that she was the one God wanted to use. If she went before the king on their behalf, she could plead for the reversal of the decree, but she feared approaching the fickle and brutal king. Mordecai challenged Esther, "Yet who knows whether you have come to the kingdom for such a time as this?" (Esther 4:14). His hopes were realized when Esther boldly approached the king and God used her to save the Jews. Instead of Haman causing the death of the Jews, the Jews caused his death and the death of his ten sons (Esther 7:10; 9:14).

When you see a particular appointment on your calendar, ask, "Are they here and am I here for such a time as this?" That is, has God allowed and divinely orchestrated the appointment because He wants you to share the gospel? Our sovereign God may have arranged this appointment so that you would share the Savior. Even if the person does not trust Christ that day, the appointment may have been arranged by God to bring him one step closer to the Kingdom. How exciting to realize you may be part of a master plan!

Don't take your appointments lightly. The one coming up may have been divinely arranged as part of His plan to bring an unbeliever to Christ.

TIP #28

INTERPRET THE SCRIPTURES ACCURATELY AND CAREFULLY.

Take God's Word Seriously

Those who are passionate about evangelism sometimes adopt methods and motives over the years that aren't biblical. Perhaps a mentor passed them along or a misunderstanding of the Bible created faulty thinking. Just as we must continuously go back to the Bible to examine our beliefs against what it says in any area, so we must in evangelism. All methods and motives, even if they seem effective and come from passion, must be held to God's word.

For example, some say, "Unless you are willing to turn from your sins, you can't be saved." This is not true, because it cannot be found in Scripture. You have to admit you are a sinner, but only after coming to Him do you have the strength and ability to say no to sin and yes to God. As Galatians 5:16 tells us, "I say then: Walk in the Spirit, and you shall not fulfill the lust of the flesh." A person must first receive the Spirit in order to walk by Him. He simply asks us to come to Him, and then *He* will help us live the life He wants us to live.

Here's another example of what some say: "If you are afraid to evangelize, you don't love Jesus." This is also not true, because it cannot be found in Scripture. A lover and proclaimer of Jesus like Paul the apostle was sometimes afraid to evangelize. When Paul entered Corinth to evangelize, he testified, "I was with you in weakness, in fear, and in much trembling" (1 Corinthians 2:3).

Paul said to his young disciple Timothy, "Be diligent to present yourself approved to God, a worker who does not need to be ashamed, rightly dividing the word of truth" (2 Timothy 2:15). Later he said, "But you be watchful in all things, endure afflictions, do the work of an evangelist, fulfill your ministry" (2 Timothy 4:5). We cannot separate careful Bible study and evangelism. They need to go together. To be effective in evangelism and most importantly approach it from God's perspective, we need to know what the Bible teaches.

God's word must govern everything we say and teach in evangelism, including our message, methods, and motives. We must always ask, "Does the Bible actually teach that?" If what we are communicating is in line with Scripture, we should not just say it, but shout it. We have the authority of God behind us. If it is not in keeping with Scripture, don't even whisper it.

The authority of God is an awesome claim. Whatever we are saying or teaching in evangelism, we need to be certain it's His word, not ours.

TIP #29

DON'T TAKE CLOSED DOORS ON YOUR SHOULDERS.

When Every Attempt Fails

Ever come up with something that you really want to do and just can't do it? It's even more frustrating when you know that your idea is honoring to God and could have eternal results.

A good example is the opportunity to share the gospel. Someone may be of such concern to you that you've asked God for boldness. You've sensed the courage to speak up that you know has come from Him, but every attempt fails. The person on your heart has not just closed the door, he or she has slammed it shut, and made it abundantly clear that you are not welcome to again discuss spiritual things.

Here, though, is where we often make our mistake. We take that problem, that reaction on our shoulders, which only leads to frustration, discouragement, self-condemnation, and sometimes anger. Instead, we need to step back and recognize that it's God's responsibility to open doors to the gospel. We don't open doors. We only walk through the ones that He has opened. Closed doors are His responsibility, not ours.

That's when Philippians 4:6 becomes a tremendous source of comfort. "Be anxious for nothing, but in everything by prayer and supplication, with thanksgiving, let your requests be made known to God." Two words are profoundly encouraging, *nothing* and *everything*. Be anxious for *nothing* and bring *everything* before Him. That includes our frustration with closed doors in evangelism. That frustration needs to be given to Him.

With that understood, keep in mind three things. First, we're dealing in the realm of spiritual things. People don't see their need until God shows it to them. Second, God alone can reach them. He has power and ability far beyond our capabilities. Third, always remember that as God works, a person who is closed today could be wide open tomorrow. Should the person have a sudden brush with death, be laid off work, or experience some other hardship or tragedy, he may be as open tomorrow as he was closed today. Should a door not open, that is still God's responsibility, not yours.

Yes, closed doors are a problem, but they are His problem, not yours. Leave them where God puts them—on His shoulders. Don't take them on yours. Your shoulders were never designed to carry that burden.

TIP #30

BE CERTAIN GOD ALWAYS GETS THE CREDIT.

Not You but Him

There's no limit to how much God can use us if we're certain God gets the credit. To do God's work, we have to set aside our own pride and desire for acknowledgement. If we're not careful, we can be led astray by the applause and comments of others.

When people in the Corinthian church started to applaud one church leader over another, Paul reminded them of two things. First, we are all servants of the living God. "Who then is Paul, and who *is* Apollos, but ministers through whom you believed, as the Lord gave to each one?" (1 Corinthians 3:5).

The second thing he told them is that God—not man—gives the increase. Paul continued by summarizing what happened: "I planted, Apollos watered, but God gave the increase" (1 Corinthians 3:6). God used Paul to start the church and Apollos's teaching to build on what Paul did, and the church grew. It was God, not Paul or Apollos, who gave the increase.

Now what may have happened had Paul and Apollos concentrated on the comments of the Corinthians? Envy and jealousy could have resulted and the ministry in Corinth could have suffered. Instead they kept the focus where it needed to be: God.

Just do what God calls you to do and let *God* prosper the work. After all, He's the one who causes a work to grow. You are just one of the ones He is using. He deserves all the credit.

Well-meaning but unfortunately not clear-thinking Christians can lead you astray. They can draw your focus to someone else receiving the credit for a conversion when you were actually the one who led that person to Christ. They may mention how someone seems to prefer another person's gift in ministry over yours. They may comment that too few seem appreciative of all you did to see a work of God grow. A friend might remark that you did not get enough recognition for all you did to make the last outreach event a success. You may feel that your financial contribution to a ministry overseas was not applauded enough.

If you fail to stay above that, Satan can cause division, turmoil, conflict, jealousy, and all the damage he's known for causing. Keep your focus where it needs to be. Ultimately, God gives the increase, so let Him have the credit. Besides, what recognition we do deserve but do not receive, He will acknowledge in heaven and give an eternal reward.

TIP #31

IF YOU ARE PRAYING FOR SOMEONE'S SALVATION, EXPECT IT TO HAPPEN.

What Did You Expect?

Some passages in the Bible are humorous. They remind us so much of ourselves. In Acts 12, Peter was thrown in prison for his faith. His fellow believers did the right thing. They prayed. Acts 12:5 tells us, "Peter was therefore kept in prison, but constant prayer was offered to God for him by the church." God answered their prayers in a miraculous way. He sent an angel to take Peter's chains from him and escort him out of prison.

Immediately, Peter ran to those who had prayed for him. Acts 12:12 says, "he came to the house of Mary, the mother of John whose surname was Mark, where many were gathered together praying." When a person named Rhoda answered the door, she was so excited she never welcomed him in. Overtaken by hearing his voice outside she "ran in and announced that Peter stood before the gate" (Acts 12:14).

This is where it gets humorous. "But they said to her, 'You are beside yourself!' Yet she kept insisting that it was so. So they said, 'It is his angel.' Now Peter continued knocking; and when they opened the door and saw him, they were astonished" (Acts 12:15–16).

You would've thought that their fervent prayers were an indication of their expectation. After all, not only is He a prayer-answering God, He is an awesome God who can do "exceedingly abundantly above all that we ask or think" (Ephesians 3:20). Instead, they were *astonished*.

It is hard to be critical of them, isn't it? We are so much like them. We pray for a lost relative but harbor doubts that they will ever come to Christ. We ask God to give us an open door and are *astonished* when He provides an opportunity sooner than expected. We ask God to give us wisdom in knowing how to respond to particular objections to the gospel. We experience His answer and tell others, "I couldn't believe it." Even in my personal experience, He has caused a response to come to my mind that I would have never thought of on my own. I've asked God for needed funds for an evangelistic outreach and then been surprised when He supplied above what was needed. In churches, we pray that there will be a great response to an evangelistic message but do not prepare to follow up with those who respond. It appears we were praying but not expecting a response.

Praying for rain? Carry an umbrella. Praying in evangelism? Expect results. Instead of being astonished, you will say, "Just what I expected."

TIP #32

GOD CAN USE US WHEN WE ARE NOT LIVING FOR HIM BUT HE CAN USE US MORE WHEN WE ARE.

A Crooked Arrow

I've never forgotten the confused look on his face. A friend informed me that a prominent pastor in his town had just confessed to having a long-time romance outside of his marriage. The pastor was a person respected for having a heart for unbelievers. The church was filled with people he had personally led to Christ. My friend wanted to know how God could use a person who is living in such an adulterous relationship.

I passed along a truth using the same words that I heard another speaker use: "God can use a crooked arrow to reach His mark." Well said! God can work in spite of us and He has. God can use a "crooked arrow." However, that is not the way He prefers to work. Besides, although He may use us while we are living in sin, our sin severely limits us. No one living in blatant disobedience experiences enablement from God to the fullest degree possible. The person's life may be the channel for the Lord's blessing, but that channel has a sizable block preventing the uninterrupted flow of the Holy Spirit.

As we evangelize, Psalm 19:12–14 needs to be our prayer. The psalmist asks of God,

> Cleanse me from secret faults.
> Keep back your servant also from presumptuous sins;
> let them not have dominion over me.
> Then I shall be blameless,
> and I shall be innocent of great transgression.

Let the words of my mouth and the meditation
  of my heart
be acceptable in Your sight,
O Lord, my strength and my Redeemer.

The psalmist wants to be delivered from both hidden faults and presumptuous sins. He cries out to the one who is his rock, the one who has delivered him from slavery to sin. His desire is that all that he says and all that he desires may be acceptable in God's sight.

Scripture and experience verify how mightily God can work through a person who in every area of his life says no to sin and yes to God. He can and does use those whose hearts are not right with Him. But don't offer to God a crooked arrow. Give Him what He desires to use—a straight one. Give Him a life that in every area is seeking to obey and know Him. That is the kind of life that has the greatest impact on the lost.

TIP #33

GOD IS PLEASED WHEN YOU TELL HIM THE STRUGGLES YOU ARE HAVING WITH HIM.

Tell Him How You Feel

In general and in evangelism particularly, the Christian life presents us with so many frustrations. Why, as we attempt to do what is right, do we struggle to make ends meet? Yet the wicked, who are so deceitful, seem to prosper beyond belief. Why are more things going wrong than right when after years of disobedience, we've finally gotten our act together with the Lord? Why does God not open the heart of a dying friend for whom we've prayed for years? Why do I always seem to meet those who are so closed to the gospel while others meet those who are so open? Why doesn't He use me the same way He seems to use others?

When those thoughts and frustrations hit us, we should do what Job in the Bible did—tell God precisely how we feel, not holding anything back. We may have to walk on eggshells with others, but we don't have to do so with God.

Job's whole world turned upside down within days. Family, possessions, health—he lost them all. Even his closest friends turned out to be his worst enemies as they gave him pathetic counsel. They encouraged him to examine the sin in his own life when God had clearly commended his righteous living (Job 1:8; 2:3).

Job sat before the Lord and said it all. One verse alone captures his raw heart:

> Therefore I will not restrain my mouth;
> I will speak in the anguish of my spirit;
> I will complain in the bitterness of my soul. (Job 7:11)

What did God do? He didn't tell Job how disappointed He was in him or what a pathetic person he was. He didn't even threaten Job with punishment for having said or felt what he claimed. God gave him time to work through his emotions, recognize the sovereignty of God, and rethink the thoughts he'd had. Then He commended Job for speaking "what is right" and rebuked Job's friends for their untruthful counsel (Job 42:7–8). God was clearly pleased with Job's honesty and integrity of heart.

God wants to hear your frustration and agonies as you evangelize. After all, why hold back from Him what He already knows?

The next time you feel disappointments and even bitterness for any reason, go ahead and tell Him. Let Him know where you're struggling and why. His ear is listening. His heart is caring. He didn't wipe Job off the map for telling Him how he felt and He won't do that to you, either.

PREPARE YOUR HEART
TO SHARE THE GOSPEL

TIP #34

YOUR ATTITUDE, NOT YOUR ABILITY TO ARGUE, ACCOMPLISHES THE MOST.

Something Better Than Arguing

One of the most common reasons believers today don't evangelize is that they fear they won't be able to answer objections or refute arguments. This logic equates winning an argument with evangelizing. With that kind of thinking, Christians assume that they need the skill of an attorney and the wit of a debater to evangelize.

The Bible warns against that thinking. In his letter to Timothy, Paul advises him how to respond to someone who rejects his message. He warns,

> But avoid foolish and ignorant disputes, knowing that they generate strife. And a servant of the Lord must not quarrel but be gentle to all, able to teach, patient, in humility correcting those who are in opposition, if God perhaps will grant them repentance, so that they may know the truth. (2 Timothy 2:23–25)

A humble attitude, not a hostile argument, wins over an opponent.

People are not brought to Christ through a system of logic, the articulation of an argument, or the power of persuasion. They're brought to Christ when the Holy Spirit takes the truth of the gospel, drives it home to their hearts, and causes them to come to God by faith. They're brought to Christ through what 1 Corinthians 2:4 calls the "demonstration of the Spirit and of power." That literally means the proving power of the Holy Spirit.

The time before salvation can be one of immense struggle for the non-Christian. Satan doesn't easily give up a fight. Ephesians 2:1–3 states that the lost are so enslaved by Satan, they can only do and respond as he directs. Hence, the lost need your patience, not your arguments. Many new believers have testified that one of the worst battles in their lives took place moments before they came to Christ. God desired to save them, but Satan desired to keep them. For example, I know of a man who, just before his conversion, was frustrated and irritated because of the restlessness caused by the Holy Spirit. As he interacted with a Christian friend and took out his frustrations on him, the believer responded, "I understand, just hang in there and it will gradually make sense to you." The new convert told me, "It was his patience and understanding attitude that got my attention."

The people God uses to win the lost are not those who can win arguments and outsmart non-Christians. They are people who allow the Holy Spirit to speak through their humble attitude.

TIP #35

KNOW HOW TO RESPOND WHEN SATAN INTIMIDATES YOU.

The Master Intimidator

Satan deserves a place in *The Guinness Book of World Records* for his ability to intimidate. He's the absolute best. No one surpasses him. Listen to some of his intimidation devices. He's probably tried them on you.

- "You have no business sharing Christ. Your life is such a far cry from what it should be."

- "Remember the last time you tried to evangelize? You failed miserably."

- "They're going to ask you questions you can't answer. Then what are you going to do?"

- "Everyone knows what a hot temper you have. They're really going to be impressed when you tell them you are a Christian."

- "Go ahead and talk about Christ—as long as you don't mind losing one of the best friends you've ever had."

- "What a way to waste time. You know as well as anyone that she's not interested."

What do you do? Say to Satan the same thing Christ did in Mark 8:33, "Get behind Me, Satan! For you are not mindful of the things of God, but the things of men." When Christ predicted His death and resurrection, Peter found it hard to accept. Peter rebuked the Savior for His words. Christ knew that those thoughts came from Satan, not Peter, because His death and resurrection were all part of God's plan. Satan placed the desires of men in Peter's mind, not the desires of God.

When Satan intimidates you in evangelism, he's doing something similar—causing you to focus on what men desire, not on what God desires. Satan is expressing what is on his mind, not what is on God's mind. Tell Satan, "Get behind me. Your thoughts are the thoughts of men, not God." Your life may not be what it should be, but God uses imperfect instruments. You may fail miserably, but you learn from your mistakes. If they ask questions you can't answer, it's no sin to say, "I don't know." Always value your friendships, but true friendship means you're even more concerned that they know Christ. They may appear disinterested, but go ahead and talk to them. You might be surprised.

Recognize intimidation for what it is and Satan for who he is. Be quick to tell him, "Get behind me, Satan. I am going to evangelize. I am about what God desires, not what you desire." After all, you are a disciple of Christ, not a disciple of Satan. Follow the Master, not the master intimidator.

TIP #36

A DEFENSIVE ATTITUDE WILL PREVENT YOU FROM BEING A BETTER WITNESS.

Pushback Helps

Let me ask you a question, but be as honest as you can, answering the way someone who knows you would answer for you. If someone has a suggestion about an area where you can improve in evangelism, how would you receive his suggestion? Are you known for your rebuttal or your receptiveness?

If the answer is your rebuttal, you lose. If your answer is your receptiveness, you win.

Why? Because pushback or feedback in evangelism can only make you a better witness. Often what someone has to offer is valid and helpful. Even if they're wrong for any reason in the pushback they give, you're still wise to give it consideration. An aspect of what they are saying could have some merit. If their pushback is invalid, then at least you know why you're discarding it.

Proverbs contains advice that may strike you as rather blunt, but God in His Word sometimes speaks bluntly because He loves deeply. Proverbs 12:1 reads, "Whoever loves instruction loves knowledge, but he who hates correction is stupid." You read it correctly. The Bible described a certain type of person as stupid!

A wise person knows the value of discipline and instruction. Hence, a person who doesn't receive such instruction or reprimand well is stupid. He has not profited in the least from what someone has to say. He has missed out on an opportunity to learn and grow. He has actually done himself great harm.

Think of an area of evangelism where people might offer you suggestions. Perhaps you try to turn a conversation to spiritual things too quickly or too slowly! Maybe something about your demeanor makes people wonder if you really care about them. Could it be that you are too impatient when someone disagrees with you? Does anger for their lost condition come through clearly, instead of compassion? Whatever it is, don't get defensive. You could overlook instruction that would improve your evangelistic skills. Receiving instruction without being defensive helps you become a better witness.

Remember something critical—a person who criticizes you is criticizing something about your idea or approach, *not* criticizing you as a person. Just as you like to give ideas to someone that will help them improve, they are trying to do the same.

So when someone offers you feedback to anything you are doing in evangelism (or any area), don't respond, "But wait a minute." Instead, say, "Thank you." One way or another, you'll be a better witness because of it.

TIP #37

YOUR PAST MISTAKES IN ANY AREA DO NOT NEED TO HOLD YOU BACK IN EVANGELISM.

The Past Is behind You

I've discovered that many sincere believers want to be stronger witnesses for Christ. They want to share the good news with consistency. But they often torment themselves with things related to their past. It may be the mess they made of their lives before they came to Christ. Or it may be the mistakes they've made in talking to others about Christ when they feel like they handled conversations poorly.

The idea of evangelism brings doubts: "What would this person think if he knew me the way God knows me?" "What if they knew as much about my bad side as my good side?" "Am I going to mess up this opportunity to evangelize the way I have before?"

There is one problem with that thinking. It represents a failure to put the past where God puts it—behind you. The Bible calls it forgiveness.

That is one reason I love Psalm 103:12, "As far as the east is from the west, so far has He removed our transgressions from us." The east and the west never meet. God promises that we will never reunite with our sins. If my sins are not on His mind, they need not be on mine either. All the times I've blown it, whether it be in my daily walk or my attempts to share the gospel, are all in the past. They could not be any further removed from His mind.

So you may have messed up in a royal way in your Christian walk. There's no better person to talk to an unbeliever about forgiveness than you, the one who has already experienced it. Sure, you still sin and make mistakes, but you are not a perfect person talking to a non-Christian. You are a sinner saved by grace pointing them to the Redeemer who can save and forgive. The issue is not how imperfect you have been, but instead how perfect He is.

For your encouragement, put yourself in the shoes of non-Christians. Would it not mean a lot to you to know that the one talking to you has failed numerous times? Yet here he is living in the joy of forgiveness he wants you to experience. You are living forgiveness, not just talking about it.

Go ahead and evangelize. You have and do mess up. Live in the spirit of forgiveness, put mistakes where they already are—behind you—and proclaim the gospel.

TIP #38

IT IS ESSENTIAL TO KNOW HOW TO HANDLE TEMPTATIONS AS YOU EVANGELIZE.

He's Been There

Caution. Evangelism can be dangerous. Among other things, it can lead to temptation. For example, if we witness to a person of the opposite sex, what starts out as pure could end up impure—an immoral relationship that was never intended. If we witness to someone who has the means to buy what he wants, not simply what he needs, the temptation to pursue material things could overwhelm the desire to pursue the lost. Paul wrote to Timothy about another believer, Demas, who got caught up with the gorgeous homes of the wealthy in Rome. Paul explained, "For Demas has forsaken me, having loved this present world" (2 Timothy 4:10). If we're not careful, the same could be said of us.

Dealing with temptation is scary, but we don't have to face it alone. Jesus has been there. Hebrews 4:15 says, "For we do not have a High Priest who cannot sympathize with our weaknesses, but was in all points tempted as we are, yet without sin." Because Jesus as He walked on earth was fully God and fully human, He experienced temptation in every area of life as we do. His temptations may not have come from sinful desires as ours do, but Satan did his best to dismantle Jesus. Having experienced Satan's best attempts to invalidate Him, Jesus can sympathize. He understands what we are going through. As our High Priest, Christ now sits at the right hand of God (Hebrews 1:3), ready to minister on our behalf.

What better person is there to talk to when tempted than Him? Hebrews 4 continues, "Let us therefore come boldly to the throne of grace, that we may obtain mercy and find grace to help in time of need" (v. 16). Come to him in prayer and find an unlimited resource of whatever is needed. Are you tempted to alter your priorities? Talk to Him. He's been there. Are you tempted to be immoral? Talk to Him. He knows the pain and seriousness of temptation. Tempted toward wrong thoughts? Talk to Him. He understands your struggle. Have you given into temptation? Talk to Him. In His mercy, He'll hold back what you do deserve and in His grace, He'll give you what you don't deserve. His supply of both mercy and grace is available whenever and wherever we need it.

Whatever temptation you face, don't walk to the throne of grace. Run to it. Boldly tell Him what it is that you need.

TIP #39

CONFRONT SATAN IN EVANGELISM; DON'T RUN FROM HIM.

Put Up a Fight

Want to get Satan mad and see his blood pressure rise? Do something in evangelism. Notice, I didn't say pray about evangelism. Prayer is essentiasl in evangelism, but there is something that can disturb Satan even more. It's when you put feet to those prayers and do something about them. By evangelizing, you are making a direct attack against his kingdom. Should the person you're witnessing to trust Christ, they are instantly transferred from the kingdom of darkness into the kingdom of light (Colossians 1:13).

That's why individuals in churches face such satanic opposition when they evangelize. It may come in the form of temptation, discouragement, fear, closed doors, or physical obstacles of one sort or another. The obstacles Satan uses are numerous. Satan absolutely detests individuals who want to be a strong witness for Christ in their families, to their neighbors, in their workplaces, or wherever they go.

What might the believer do? Follow the advice James gives. Speaking to believers who are living closer to the world than they are to Christ, he gives them the same remedy we need when Satan tries to thwart evangelism: "Resist the devil and he will flee from you" (James 4:7).

Take a stand against the devil. The situation will determine what that stand looks like. No matter what temptation Satan throws our way, there is always a way of escape (1 Corinthians 10:13). You're never the victim of his devices. If he uses discouragement, fill your mind with the good you have seen happen as you evangelize (Philippians 4:8). If he uses fear, recognize the power of prayer and do what Paul the apostle did—ask God for boldness (Ephesians 6:19–20). If he provokes ridicule, count it an honor to suffer for His sake (Philippians 1:29). If he provokes resentment, ask God to help you forgive the resentful the way He forgave you (Colossians 3:13).

What will happen? "He will flee from you" (James 4:7). Satan is Satan, but he's not stupid. Time and effort can be better used elsewhere than trying to thwart the efforts of those who refuse to submit to his devices. In other words, instead of Satan being a discouragement to you, you become a discouragement to him.

When we take a stand, we do so through His strength, not ours. But keep in mind that, "He who is in you is greater than he who is in the world" (1 John 4:4). So instead of running from Satan, take a stand and let *him* run from *you*.

TIP #40

KNOWING HOW TO HANDLE ANY STRUGGLE ABOUT YOUR OWN SALVATION IS CRITICAL IN EVANGELIZING.

Struggles Are Beneficial

Struggles are difficult. But sometimes they are beneficial. A person I know struggled with throat cancer. As horrible as it was, he told me, "It made me a more compassionate person."

On the one hand nothing is worse than struggling about your salvation. Among other things, how do you speak to someone about their salvation if you are not sure of your own? At the same time responding to those struggles properly may be the spiritually-healthiest thing you have ever done. In responding correctly you may realize why you can be as certain of your future address (heaven) as you are of your present one. It will also help you to help others.

Let's start here. On what basis does God guarantee your salvation? The biblical answer is "Have you trusted Christ?" In John 6:47 Christ declared, "Most assuredly, I say to you, he who believes in Me has everlasting life." *Believe* has the idea of trust, dependence, and reliance. We have to come to God as sinners and recognize that two thousand years ago Jesus Christ paid for our sins by dying as our substitute. The third day He arose. When we place our trust in Christ alone to save us, He gives us the completely free gift of eternal life. He gives you what He promises to give you the moment you trust Christ.

So the question is, "Are you trusting Christ alone as your only way to heaven?" It's not when or where you made a decision that matters. Some know the date, others don't. It's that you are trusting Christ and Christ alone as your only way to everlasting life, your only means to a right standing with God.

But if we address that struggle the wrong way we will only confuse ourselves. For example, some ask, "Am I as loving as I need to be?" "What is my prayer life like?" "Do I always act like a Christian?" Assurance of salvation is not based on your performance. It's based on *His* performance when He died as your substitute. You're saved because you accepted His sacrifice on your behalf. Everything else is part of *growing* as a Christian, not *becoming* a Christian.

When you struggle about your salvation, let those struggles benefit you. Determine if you are saved and why from a biblical perspective. Your struggle with your salvation will become a thing of the past. Having settled your own struggle in this area, you can help others settle theirs.

TIP #41

LIVING THE PROPER LIFE BEFORE UNBELIEVERS IS NOT ENOUGH.

Show but Don't Forget to Share

This common saying has been attributed to different people: "Witness to everyone you can; if necessary use words." Although well intended, the saying has no biblical or practical support.

Sure, your life should *attract* people to the Savior, but someone has to speak to them. That's why the Bible tells us to be witnesses. Acts 1:8 says, "But you shall receive power when the Holy Spirit has come upon you; and you shall be witnesses to Me in Jerusalem, and in all Judea and Samaria, and to the end of the earth." A witness is someone who tells what he knows, what he has personally experienced. How can you tell someone what you know without talking to them?

Now think of it from a purely practical level. You may live the most Christlike life of anyone on the planet. I can stare at you as you live that life. But as I stare at you, I have no idea *how* to come to Christ. Yes, I have noticed something different about you, but I still don't know how to attain that something for myself. Unless someone explains to me that 1) I'm a sinner who deserves to be eternally separated from God, 2) Christ died for me and rose again, and 3) I have to trust Christ alone to save me, I have no idea how to come to Christ.

Who may be tempted to use that saying about witnessing? Two people. The first is someone who is concerned that Christians live the life they should, a life that causes others to say, "Whatever she has, I want it." While that concern is valid, we need to be careful that we don't respond by saying something that has no biblical or practical truth to it.

A second person would be the one who is fearful of speaking to others about Christ. That fear may be the fear of not knowing how to turn a conversation to spiritual things, the fear of not knowing how to present the gospel, the fear of not knowing how to answer objections, or the fear of rejection. Such a saying intentionally or unintentionally becomes an excuse behind which a person hides to shirk responsibility.

Learn how to evangelize and there will be no need to use such a statement. You will be confident in speaking to unbelievers and you will want to share with them the most important message of the Bible—salvation by grace through faith.

There is no better combination of evangelism than show and share. Show them Christ *and* share Him with them.

TIP #42

THE ABILITY TO LISTEN IS MORE IMPORTANT THAN THE ABILITY TO TALK.

Are You Listening?

Read through the book of Proverbs. As you do, note how many times Proverbs emphasizes that wise people listen.

"A wise man will hear and increase learning" (1:5).

"My son, hear the instruction of your father" (1:8).

"But whoever listens to me will dwell safely" (1:33).

"So that you incline your ear to wisdom" (2:2).

"Hear, my children, the instruction of a father" (4:1).

"Hear, my son, and receive my sayings" (4:10).

"My son, give attention to my words; incline your ear to my sayings" (4:20).

Again and again, one hears Proverbs shouting: Listen! Listen! Listen!

In evangelism, listening is key. It's safe to say that the ear matters more than the tongue.

What does listening do? It shows you how to turn a conversation to spiritual things. As you talk about topics such as their families, jobs, and backgrounds, you find places you can relate to them and build a personalized bridge to the gospel. For example, they may talk about their family vacations to national parks and all of the beauty they enjoyed. That may give you a chance to remark, "I'm like you. I like nature. The more I look at creation, the more I'm convinced there must be a Creator." As again you listen to their response you may ascertain any interest in spiritual things, but it is *them* talking and you listening that presents possible openings into spiritual matters. It is the ear that teaches you what to say.

People often come to Christ in the midst of a crisis—something that causes feelings of hurt, disappointment, or insecurity. It may be the loss of a mate, a job, their health, or finances. Listening, not talking, tells you where and how they are hurting. Listening also tells them that you care. People who are hurting need someone who listens more than someone who talks. Minutes spent listening ministers far more than minutes spent talking.

Listening also teaches you how fast to proceed. As you ask them questions you determine where they are spiritually and what particular reservations or objections they may have to the gospel. Even if time and circumstances do not allow you to present the gospel, your listening may tell you where to start next time and even how to pray for them in the meantime.

Listen! Those effective in evangelism are not those who have developed the art of using their tongue but those who have developed the art of using their ears.

TIP #43

LEARN FROM OTHERS WHO HAVE DEVELOPED SKILLS THAT COULD BE HELPFUL TO YOU.

Don't Discount Someone Who Has Traveled ahead of You

Think of areas of your life where you have grown the most. Now think of particular people who helped you grow in those areas. Who were they? What was the common denominator about them? Chances are they were people who walked down the path ahead of you, went through similar experiences, and learned what you are just now learning.

The same principle is true in evangelism. One of the ways you develop your skills is by learning from someone with the gift of evangelism who has already developed his skills. A person with the gift of evangelism has the ability to present not only the gospel but also to equip others to do the same. That is why we are told in Ephesians 4:11–12, "And He Himself gave some *to be* apostles, some prophets, some evangelists, and some pastors and teachers, for the equipping of the saints for the work of ministry, for the edifying of the body of Christ."

But the one teaching you to reach others does not necessarily have to be a person gifted in evangelism. Proverbs 27:17 says, "As iron sharpens iron, so a man sharpens the countenance of his friend." When two people interact with each other, they grow together and sharpen one another's ability. While seeking development from someone with the gift of evangelism is one option, don't limit yourself. Perhaps you know someone who claims no such gift, but seems more confident in evangelism than you are. Undoubtedly, he has learned some things along the way that have helped him greatly. Let him teach you what experience has taught him.

Don't stop there either. "Iron sharpens iron" can have a wide range of possibilities. Perhaps you know someone who is in the sales field and is good at meeting strangers, initiating conversations, and introducing his products. What is it about his words and demeanor that make a person feel relaxed and eager to share? What is it about the way she approaches people that makes you feel like you have met a friend? What is it about the way he speaks that makes you feel free to ask questions? Any observations you have made in watching others interact might be helpful to you in evangelism.

More than one skill is involved in presenting the gospel. These relate to developing rapport, turning conversations, relaxing fears, and showing concern for others. When someone develops skills that could be beneficial to you in evangelizing the lost, let their strengths become yours.

TIP #44

PEOPLE MATTER A LOT MORE THAN POSSESSIONS.

It's About Who, Not What

I am often asked the question, "What will help keep me focused on reaching lost people?" There is more than one answer to that question, but there is also another factor we too quickly overlook.

One of the things I tell people is that when you jump out of bed in the morning, remember a simple principle: possessions pass, people last. Everyone faces eternity either with God or without God. Those with God experience eternal life, a joy that cannot be overstated. Those separated from God experience eternal condemnation, a torment that is often understated. John 3:36 explains, "He who believes in the Son has everlasting life; and he who does not believe the Son shall not see life, but the wrath of God abides on him."

Materialism often keeps us from prioritizing evangelism and even using our resources for Christ. Subtly it creeps up on us and takes control of our lives. We get too focused on the here and now. Goods and gadgets, luxury items of one sort or another in their rightful place are not inherently bad. In the wrong place they take priority over people. Our time, energy, attitudes, and resources go to all the things that one hundred years from now won't even matter.

Second Peter 3:10–12 keeps us on track. We read,

But the day of the Lord will come as a thief in the night, in which the heavens will pass away with a great noise, and the elements will melt with fervent heat; both the earth and the works that are in it will be burned up. Therefore, since all these things will be dissolved, what manner of persons ought you to be in holy conduct and godliness, looking for and hastening the coming of the day of God, because of which the heavens will be dissolved, being on fire, and the elements will melt with fervent heat?

When the Lord returns the "heavens will pass away with a great noise, and the elements will melt with fervent heat." Everything is gone. Only people will last. The text asks, "What matter of persons ought we to be in holy conduct and godliness?" One aspect of godliness is sharing His love for the lost and His good news with them. It's being a fisher of men (Matthew 4:19). Should they come to Christ, they will be there with us. If they don't, they suffer eternal separation from Him.

Remember: possessions pass, people last.

TIP #45

WHAT YOUR ENEMY NEEDS MOST FROM YOU IS THE GOOD NEWS OF THE GOSPEL.

The Best Treatment of an Enemy

A believer once told me, "I really don't want to witness to him. I really don't care if he goes to hell." He was speaking candidly of someone who had treated him hatefully. But then he added something that spoke loudly of his character, or I should say, of his obedience: "But I'm going to because I realize he needs Christ. Besides, that's what God wants me to do."

Witnessing to those you like is relatively easy. Witnessing to those you don't like is often difficult.

That is precisely what we need to do. Jesus said,

> "You have heard that it was said, 'You shall love your neighbor and hate your enemy.' But I say to you, love your enemies, bless those who curse you, do good to those who hate you, and pray for those who spitefully use you and persecute you." (Matthew 5:43–44)

The scribes and Pharisees were discriminating in loving others, but Jesus did not teach to hate enemies as they did. Christ taught that one of the ways we resemble God the most is when we love "whosoever." By doing so, "you may be sons of your Father in heaven; for He makes His sun rise on the evil and on the good, and sends rain on the just and on the unjust" (v. 45). If God's love has no boundaries, ours shouldn't either.

With that in mind, what is the absolute best way we could ever love our enemy? The answer is to share the good news of the gospel with them.

Why does that kind of love make us more Christlike? We are loving the people who are undeserving of our love, just as we were undeserving of His. The Bible even says that apart from Christ, we are His "enemies." Romans 5:10 tells us that "when we were enemies we were reconciled to God through the death of His Son." So if God would love us when we were His enemies, we are obedient and Christlike when we love those who we regard as our enemies. We are loving them in their condition just as God loved us when we were in the same condition.

God gave us what we don't deserve—an invitation to eternal life. Even if it is someone you regard as your enemy, go and do likewise (Luke 10:37). It is the obedient thing to do and the best thing you can do for them.

TIP #46

INVEST FINANCIALLY IN EVANGELISM, THEN LET YOUR HEART FOLLOW YOUR MONEY.

Money Matters

Committed believers want to keep on track in evangelism. They don't want to lose their focus on the lost. They desire an ever-increasing passion to spread the good news of the gospel. What they often overlook is that there is one simple thing that will help them in that area: money.

No one understood that better than Christ, nor did anyone say it more succinctly. While discussing the need to lay up treasures that last instead of treasures that pass, Christ laid out a very simple principle to his listeners that would impact the rest of their lives and keep them on track. He said, "For where your treasure is, there your heart will be also" (Matthew 6:21). Your heart always follows what you treasure, not vice versa. Your heart follows your money.

The ramifications of that are seen every day, aren't they? Why are some churches so foreign-mission minded? Because they send a large portion of what comes in overseas. They even encourage their people to go on short-term mission trips to particular fields to see what their funds are accomplishing. Why do some parents become concerned about a university's standards or programs? Because they've given much toward the school's growth or even underwritten the educational expense of one of their students, often one of their own family members. Even after the student graduates, they often continue to support the school financially, because they have a heart for it. Why do some people take pride in a new home or new car? Large portions of their annual income secured both and they want to guard carefully what cost them much.

So how can money keep you on track in evangelism? Take a significant portion of your income and give it toward a ministry that does nothing but reach the lost. Each month you'll be reminded that Christ came to seek and save the lost. Help a non-Christian family facing a hardship over which they had no control, but one that only money will resolve. Besides having a part of your money, they'll have a part of your heart. Give a non-Christian a gift they otherwise could not enjoy. Your sacrifice will not only touch them, it will also touch you.

Let money keep you on track in evangelism. Put some treasure into the lost and witness the outcome—a heart and a life that stays focused on non-Christians.

TIP #47

MAKE A LIST OF WHAT SATAN COULD USE TO DESTROY YOUR WITNESS.

Be on the Alert

The Bible has a reason for calling Satan the devil. He is subtle, vicious, lustful, deceptive, prideful, divisive, hateful, murderous, and accusatory. He will stop at nothing to accomplish his evil purposes. Even when he appears to be on the side of righteousness, it is a cover-up for his wicked ways.

Paul the apostle knew to be on the alert for Satan's devices. He testified, "lest Satan should take advantage of us; for we are not ignorant of his devices" (2 Corinthians 2:11). Paul must have spent time thinking about how Satan might divert him and prepared himself accordingly.

Satan would love to get anyone in evangelism off track. Be wise! Stop and think for a moment what Satan could use in your life.

For some it is immorality. Satan causes one to neglect what the Bible says about fleeing sexual immorality (1 Corinthians 6:18) and thus fall victim to his temptations. It doesn't happen overnight. Week by week Satan causes the believer to let down his guard. A wholesome relationship can then easily become an immoral one. Feelings overtake common sense. A once-effective witness for Christ now has a polluted testimony.

For others it is greed. First Timothy 6:10 warns us, "For the love of money is a root of all *kinds of* evil, for which some have strayed from the faith in their greediness, and pierced themselves through with many sorrows." Satan could not stand the way a person was blessed materially, so he decided to take the blessing and turn it into a curse. Instead of the believer owning much, everything he had began to own him. Possessions became more important than people. His earthly wealth became more important than preparing people for the hereafter.

Sometimes Satan uses what Paul referred to in 2 Corinthians 2:10—a lack of forgiveness. We've experienced Godly forgiveness; the problem is we can't forgive others. Ever try to evangelize when your heart is filled with so much bitterness that you'd rather see people punished than pardoned?

Make a list of what Satan could use or do in your life. Now what can you do to prepare against his attack? Have an accountability partner? Change a daily routine or habit? Refuse to meet with someone under certain circumstances? There *is* a way to prepare against his attack. Do it! You, not Satan, become the victor.

TIP #48

IMITATE CHRIST THROUGH YOUR CONTACTS AND COMPASSION.

New Converts Have What We Sometimes Lose

New believers can teach us a lot, including the importance of keeping two things we are prone to lose.

One is contacts. Their world is made up of people who don't know the Lord. After all, that is the world they were saved out of. Statistically, after we've been converted for about two years, we've dropped most of our non-Christian friends. How do we maintain contact with the lost?

The second is compassion. New believers are often so excited about their newfound relationship with Christ that they want all their friends to come to Christ, too, so much so that sometimes concern overwhelms tact. In what's considered a fairly abrupt way, they confront those they know with their need of Christ. Often though, and sadly, we lose that compassion for unbelievers. Although we want non-Christians to come to Christ, sometimes we have little or no urgency in sharing the gospel with them. I am commonly asked, "What do you do if you feel like you've lost your compassion for the lost?"

The answer is contained in two words: imitate Christ. Paul said in 1 Corinthians 11:1, "Imitate me, just as I also imitate Christ." A superb place to find out what will happen when you imitate Christ is Luke 19:1–10, the familiar story of Jesus and Zaccheus.

Jesus had contact with the lost. Imagine how many homes He walked past that day as He entered and passed through Jericho so that He might enter the home of a sinner who so desperately needed Him. As He saw Zaccheus perched in a tree, He said, "Zaccheus, make haste and come down, for today I must stay at your house" (v. 5). Are you willing to decline time spent with Christians, if necessary, to instead spend time with the lost?

But why did He give this invitation? Because He had compassion and was concerned about Zaccheus's eternal condition. He specifically said, "for the Son of Man has come to seek and to save that which was lost" (v. 10). Imitating Christ means there are other things that might burden you about lost people, such as the situation with their family, finances, or health. But the thing that should burden you the most is that they are lost and without hope, destined to a Christless eternity.

Imitate Christ and you won't lose the two things that often characterize new believers—contact and compassion. In fact, the closer you come to Him, the more you will find those two to be on the increase, not the decrease.

TIP #49

OUTSIDE OF CHRIST, UNBELIEVERS HAVE NOTHING.

Don't Envy Unbelievers

Sometimes God uses foolish people to teach us. Zophar in the book of Job is a good illustration. In Job 20, he is counseling Job as to why he had lost everyone and everything. Zophar concluded that God caused Job's plight as the consequence of his "wickedness" (v. 29). I am sure had you been in Job's shoes you would have felt like saying, "With friends like you, who needs enemies?" After all, God Himself applauded Job's righteous character and conduct (Job 1:8).

But out of that wrong counsel, Zophar makes an interesting observation. He states it rather bluntly and sarcastically (because he is including Job among the wicked) but at least it is the truth. He says,

> "Do you *not* know this of old,
> Since man was placed on earth,
> That the triumphing of the wicked is short,
> And the joy of the hypocrite is *but* for a moment?
> Though his haughtiness mounts up to the heavens,
> And his head reaches to the clouds,
> *Yet* he will perish forever like his own refuse;
> Those who have seen him will say, 'Where is he?'
> He will fly away like a dream, and not be found;
> Yes, he will be chased away like a vision of the night.
> The eye *that* saw him will *see him* no more,
> Nor will his place behold him anymore." (Job 20:4–9)

The word "refuse" may be translated "dung." The time wicked people have is short and they perish like dung. Their life and their successes are here today, gone tomorrow. The way this should affect us personally and should affect our evangelism is powerful. As we see all that unbelievers have obtained (sometimes deceitfully), we must realize they have it for a small amount of time. Sixty-five, seventy, perhaps ninety or ninety-five years, and it's all over and gone. Any happiness attached to it is also short-lived.

For the believer the party only *begins* when we see Him face-to-face. Our happiness increases as we look forward to eternity with Christ. Unbelievers' happiness not only decreases, but it ends. When you see things from that biblical perspective, it makes you pity unbelievers. It also motivates you to share Christ with them. As believers we have everything. As unbelievers, biblically speaking, they have nothing.

Pity unbelievers, don't envy them. Unless they come to know Him, they and all they have perishes like dung.

TIP #50

SHARING THE GOOD NEWS IS ONE OF THE BEST WAYS TO MEET YOUR OBLIGATION TO LOVE.

The Best Way to Say "I Love You"

The Scriptures do not encourage debt; they discourage it because you become a slave to the person from whom you borrowed (Proverbs 22:7). The Bible even says, "Owe no one anything" (Romans 13:8).

But there is one kind of debt that is encouraged, though you might call it an obligation to love. Paul speaks of this debt in Romans 13.

After speaking of the obligations we have toward those in legal authority over us, Paul expresses an obligation we have to all men. Romans 13:8 tells us, "Owe no one anything except to love one another, for he who loves another has fulfilled the law." The one obligation we should feel toward our fellow man is the need to love him. As we meet that requirement, we meet every requirement the law expresses in terms of the responsibilities we have before anyone and everyone. Love sums up how we should be toward others.

Let's take that a step further. If we sincerely love our fellow man, is there a better way to express that than to share the gospel?

Think about this. If we love them enough to tell them where they can buy the home of their dreams at a price they can afford, we have affected their happiness on earth. If we tell them of the one doctor that has been successful in curing their otherwise incurable disease, we have affected their health and maybe their longevity. If we tell them of a person who has overcome the same handicap their son suffers with, we have affected a family. If we tell them of a firm looking for their expertise and the firm hires them, we have affected their income. But in no way, as important as those are, have we impacted their eternal destiny.

What will happen if we love them enough to tell them how they can live forever with God? We will share the gospel. Should they accept His free gift, we have impacted their *eternal* home. They have received something they can never lose because the giver of that gift—God—never takes it back. Whatever changes about their lives—that is one thing that will never change. Through the way God used us, we have just made the biggest impact on them we could ever make.

So see yourself as having a major obligation, one that is very rewarding to fulfill: love others by telling them the good news of Jesus Christ.

UNDERSTAND YOUR AUDIENCE

TIP #51

BECAUSE PEOPLE DIFFER, THERE IS ONE MESSAGE BUT MANY WAYS TO EVANGELIZE.

"One Size Fits All" Does Not Work

You've seen the ads—"one size fits all." What a relief! Now I don't need to worry about whether I'm small, medium, or large. Whatever I am, the particular item is made to fit.

Sometimes we wish that were true in evangelism—one method reaches everyone. Unfortunately it's not. Methods of evangelism are as varied as people to whom we are talking.

One caution. We are not talking about the *message* we have for the lost. That never changes. Our message is that Christ died for our sins and rose from the dead (1 Corinthians 15:3–5). The means or ways by which we get the message out varies.

The New Testament not only allows us to vary our means to evangelize, but it also shows variety in one verse. Acts 5:42 reads, "And daily in the temple, and in every house, they did not cease teaching and preaching Jesus *as* the Christ." "In the temple" could be called proclamation evangelism or what is called mass evangelism. "In every house" could be called one-to-one evangelism or what is called personal evangelism. The thrust of the New Testament is, "Just get the gospel out. Christ died for our sins and rose from the dead." Use every means to get that message to any and every person.

Why are so many methods needed? The recipients of that message, lost people, are so diverse. One may be a person who hates crowds and is reluctant to attend an evangelistic event or even go to church. But a one-to-one conversation from a person who has shown interest in him may cause him to open up and respond to the gospel.

Another person is a talker, so much so that he gives you little chance to say anything. At a public gathering where the gospel is clearly explained, though, he has to sit and listen. That public proclamation of the gospel could bring him one step closer to the cross.

Still another is an avid reader. Loaning her a book that causes her to think about spiritual things may open up the door to a conversation about who Christ is and why He came.

Another acquaintance may enjoy drama. A play of some sort that acts out the gospel story may cause her to think and respond.

God saves people from all backgrounds, cultures, interest levels, and ages. "One size fits all" may work in the department store. It does not work in evangelism.

TIP #52

APPROACH UNBELIEVERS THE WAY YOU WOULD WANT THEM TO APPROACH YOU.

Think Before You Speak

Few haven't heard it: "Therefore, whatever you want men to do to you, do also to them" (Matthew 7:12). As Christ explained, in living according to this simple principle, you fulfill the life prescribed in the law and the prophets. It's often referred to as the Golden Rule. Do unto others as you would have them to do unto you.

This applies to every area of life, including our words. What we say and how we say it matters. It applies as much to our personal outreach as it does anywhere else. As we think about evangelism, we might apply it by saying, "Speak unto others as you would have them to speak unto you."

Let's look at a few scenarios. Consider how you might feel in each approach.

You are working in a tollbooth. A believer comes by after paying his toll and then shoves a tract in your face as he says, "Here, read this." Wouldn't you prefer a more personal approach? Consider handing someone a tract with these words: "I wish we had time to talk about spiritual things. Since we don't, may I share something with you that has meant a lot to me personally? I think you will enjoy it, too."

Suppose in a moment of weakness, you respond to an unbeliever in a harsh and tense tone. If you were that unbeliever, would you prefer the believer ignore what happened? The believer might be tempted to think, "In time, he'll forget it. It wasn't that big of a deal." Or would you prefer he ask for forgiveness?

As an unbeliever, you are typically seen as one who makes bad choices. As you confess one of those, would you prefer to have a believer say, "Maybe God is trying to tell you something"? Or would you prefer he say, "I know how you feel. I've made some bad choices, too. Let's talk and I'll share some of my own mistakes"?

Suppose you are an unbeliever with a poor reputation. You decide to go to church one Sunday. Would you prefer to have a believer who knows you and your reputation say, "Let me see if I can find you a seat" (as he searches for one where you are barely noticed)? Or would you prefer he invite you to sit with him and his family?

Think before you speak. Doing so will help you speak unto others the way you'd have others speak unto you. It could make an eternal difference.

TIP #53

ASSUME THAT IF THEY ARE OPEN TO YOU AS A PERSON, THEY'RE OPEN TO HEARING THE GOSPEL.

Open or Closed

Open doors in the physical realm are not hard to detect, but open doors in the spiritual realm are not quite as easy. Will the person even *want* to talk about spiritual things? They look friendly and conversational but perhaps only to a point. What if they've had an unpleasant experience with another Christian and shut you off as soon as you bring up spiritual things? How do you know if a particular person is an open or closed door when it comes to the gospel?

Two verses in Scripture offer us some guidance. First Corinthians 16:8–9 tells us, "But I will tarry in Ephesus until Pentecost. For a great and effective door has opened to me, and *there are* many adversaries." Paul was planning to leave Ephesus to visit Corinth, but despite opposition, the opportunities to minister in that major city of Asia Minor were so great he decided to stay longer.

Now examine 1 Thessalonians 2:17–18. There Paul said,

> But we, brethren, having been taken away from you for a short time in presence, not in heart, endeavored more eagerly to see your face with great desire. Therefore we wanted to come to you—even I, Paul, time and again—but Satan hindered us.

Paul had such an intense love for the believers of Thessalonica that he tried on several occasions to return to them. He wanted to provide the necessary follow-up for new converts, but Satan hindered him "time and again." We know from 1 John 4:4 that "He who is in you is greater than he who is in the world." Everything Satan does happens only through the permission of God. Although God did not hinder Paul's return, He allowed Satan to for reasons known only to Him.

Assume that an open door to you is an open door for the gospel and proceed one step at a time. One might find, like in Ephesus, the door keeps swinging wider and wider. Then one might find, like in Paul's desire to return to Thessalonica, that at this particular time the opportunity is not there.

Engage in conversation with the lost. If an unbeliever is open to you as a person, keep walking and talking. Once more, take one step at a time. Let the Holy Spirit direct you; don't try to direct Him. Let God show you through their openness to you as a person whether the door for the gospel is currently open or closed.

TIP #54

LEADING NON-CHRISTIANS, NOT ALLOWING THEM TO LEAD YOU, WILL IMPACT YOUR CREDENTIALS.

Who Is Leading Whom?

It has been said, "Christians are no different than non-Christians. They look a lot alike."

Unfortunately, that is often true. But what is the problem? Is it that Christians are spending too much time with non-Christians? The cause of the problem may be various factors, but it certainly is not that Christians are spending time with non-Christians. After all, you cannot have personal evangelism without personal contact. If you want to reach the lost, you have to spend time with the lost. Even still, though, personal contact can lead to a problem of influence—who is influencing whom?

Too often we allow our non-Christian friends to lead us instead of us leading them. We are to light the way for them to walk, not follow in the direction they are walking. Christ plainly said,

> "You are the light of the world. A city that is set on a hill cannot be hidden. Nor do they light a lamp and put it under a basket, but on a lampstand, and it gives light to all who are in the house. Let your light so shine before men, that they may see your good works and glorify your Father in heaven." (Matthew 5:14–16)

A light is not placed under a basket. A contractor does not build a city on a hill in an attempt to hide it. Instead both are placed in an elevated position, so all benefit from them. In a world darkened to sin, Christians should always stand out for the right reasons, not the wrong reasons. We offer light and point them to the One who is our Light.

The bottom line is that we should lead non-Christians, not allow them to lead us. A light illuminates and shows the path for them to walk. If we consistently live as a light, we can affect others in every room we enter. The "light" characteristic of our lives stands out wherever we go, whether to work, school, the store, or the amusement park. It should also be seen in all circumstances we run into whether we're excited or bored, feeling loved or feeling lonely, feeling well or suffering physically. That consistency characterizes our lives and gives credibility to our witness. The fact that we are different stands out in a very positive way.

As you spend time with non-Christians, who is leading whom? Are you following them or are they following you? The answer directly affects the impact you will have upon unbelievers.

TIP #55

TELL UNBELIEVERS WHAT YOU KNOW; DON'T TRY TO EXPLAIN WHAT YOU DON'T KNOW.

Proclaim What You Know

Many people come to Christ in the midst of a crisis. Loss of mate. Loss of job. Loss of home. Disabling illness. Financial reversal. Their business goes up in flames. A difficult move to another part of the country. Their security crumbles around them.

The crisis may present your best opportunity to witness to them. As never before, they seem approachable about spiritual things. One caution: be careful to tell them what you know, not what you don't know. Saying nothing could be more helpful in bringing them to God than saying the wrong thing.

Consider Job. His world had fallen apart around him. Family, possessions, and servants were all wiped out. But what added grief to grief was the way his so-called "friends" tried to help him. Take Bildad for an example. We read in Job 8:11–14,

> "Can the papyrus grow up without a marsh?
> Can the reeds flourish without water?
> While it is yet green and not cut down,
> it withers before any other plant.
> So are the paths of all who forget God;
> and the hope of the hypocrite shall perish,
> whose confidence shall be cut off,
> and whose trust is a spider's web."

Bildad thought he had the answer. It was, "Look what nature shows us. The cause of a withered plant is a lack of water.

Since you have experienced these great losses, obviously there is sin in your life. Look what happens when you forget God."

His reasoning was easy to follow, yet still very wrong. God Himself had commended Job for his godly character (Job 1:8; 2:3). There was not one ounce of truth to what Bildad was saying. Bildad would have honored God and helped Job more if he had said nothing. His comments were more harmful then helpful.

A helpful principle can be drawn from this passage. A crisis could be your God-given opportunity to reach them, but be careful with your words. Many times there is no way to explain a tragedy. You simply do not know enough. Instead, tell them what you know. Explain what God did by allowing His Son to die as their substitute, proving how much He cares for them. Through faith they can enter into a relationship with the God who cares.

Say the right thing. Tell people what you know, not what you don't know.

TIP #56

BE CAREFUL THAT PRE-EVANGELISM IS WHERE YOU START, NOT WHERE YOU STOP.

Do You Go Far Enough?

My wife and I agreed to meet close friends of ours for dinner. Just before I arrived at the restaurant, I mistakenly took the exit before the one I needed. That decision forced me to make a circle and come back around again. I was on the right road. I just hadn't driven far enough.

Sometimes we do this in evangelism. We give people physical bread but don't extend the bread of life. We give people financial help to meet their next house payment but fail to tell them of the greatest home they could ever have—an eternal residence in heaven. In essence, we are on the right road; we just don't go far enough.

Evangelism means sharing the gospel with the intent of seeing the person trust Christ. It includes information *and* invitation. Whether or not the person trusts Christ, they have been evangelized when the gospel (Christ died for our sins and rose from the dead) was explained and they have been invited to trust Christ. That is why meeting physical needs could more accurately be called pre-evangelism. In a tangible way it shows people we genuinely care about them.

In some instances pre-evangelism is more critical than others. An unbeliever may have been turned off by believers who seemed so wrapped up in their own world that they did not have time or concern to get involved in the lives of others. Another grew up in a home where religion was stuffed down his throat and was nothing more than a duty—and a most boring one. Pre-evangelism in these situations becomes central.

Christ set the example in the New Testament in the many ways He met physical needs. He knew the importance of pre-evangelism. He healed the lame man by the pool of Bethesda (John 5:1–15), fed the five thousand with five loaves and two fish (John 6:1–14), and restored sight to the blind man (John 9:1–41). Often though, meeting these physical needs authenticated who He was and became a bridge to speak to them about their spiritual need that only He could meet (John 20:30–31).

The meeting of physical needs is both warranted and biblically encouraged. We must be careful, though, to recognize that until we share the gospel at the right time and place, we have not gone far enough. We must ultimately address their spiritual need.

Meet physical needs but keep traveling. Don't stop until the pre-evangelized have been evangelized.

TIP #57

BALANCE BETWEEN RUSHING IN AND TAKING FOREVER.

Don't Be an Extremist

Have you ever noticed that one of the things we are good at is going to extremes? We do it in almost every area of life.

For example, some people are so financially stingy that they fail to reach out and help those in need when they have the resources to do so. Others are so generous that they fail to watch their budget and spend what they don't possess. Some are so committed to their family that they have little time or concern for those outside their home who need care. Others spend so much time with those outside the home that they neglect their own families.

We do the same thing in evangelism. We go to extremes. Some who evangelize wait too long to talk to an unbeliever, not seeming to recognize that tomorrow may never come. They act like coming to Christ has no urgency about it. Others rush in so fast, a non-Christian feels used and abused. Instead of being approached with the gospel, he feels attacked by the believer who is sharing the gospel.

Ephesians 5:15–16 helps us a lot. We read, "See then that you walk circumspectly, not as fools but as wise, redeeming the time, because the days are evil." In a nutshell God is saying walk sensibly and do the right thing. We need to demonstrate skillfulness in the way we live our lives before those who have not met the Savior. We wisely do everything we can to attract them to the Savior. "Redeeming the time" means making the days count because we know our days on earth are limited. We grab every opportunity we have to attract them to Christ and share the gospel.

There are those who don't seem to understand the need to gain the trust of non-Christians. Trust allows you to present the gospel as a person who has been proven reliable. This could happen in a few moments or it could take a few months. Even still, some callously plow into spiritual things without having any preliminary conversations and risk frightening or offending unbelievers.

But the other extreme are those who never confront the lost with the truth, refusing to understand the urgency. Even when the opportunity presents itself, they seem to feel that there will be another time at some point in the future.

Don't be a victim of extremes in evangelism. Make Ephesians 5:15–16 your directive, always seeking to do the right thing. Consistently seek out opportunities to advance His kingdom, mindful your days to do so will soon be over.

TIP #58

DON'T PUT OFF TILL TOMORROW SOMEONE WHO SHOULD BE APPROACHED TODAY.

Why Wait?

The week after I stayed in his home during a speaking weekend, my host passed away from a heart attack. As I spoke with his widow, she shared that the day before he died, he led his first person to Christ using what he had learned from that weekend.

We urge people to come to Christ, reminding them they are only one heartbeat from the grave. What we often forget is that *we* are also one heartbeat away. We don't know how much time we have to reach the lost and impact others for Christ.

In James 4:13–15, James addresses people who are living closer to the world than to Christ. As a result, the world has impacted their thinking instead of their thinking impacting the world. James said,

> Come now, you who say, "Today or tomorrow we will go to such and such a city, spend a year there, buy and sell, and make a profit"; whereas you do not know what will happen tomorrow. For what is your life? It is even a vapor that appears for a little time and then vanishes away. Instead you ought to say, "If the Lord wills, we shall live and do this or that."

James's audience at the time had decided everything—when they would be leaving, where they would be going, how long they would be staying, and how much they would be making.

The only thing that they didn't consider was the nature of life. As steam that comes up from a kettle and quickly dissipates, they could be here today and gone tomorrow. At most they could only say, "Lord willing, we will live and do this or that." Just like the lost are not promised tomorrow, neither are we as the believers who tell them about Christ.

How should that affect our evangelism? Whatever we can do today, we should do and refuse to wait until tomorrow. If the opportunity to visit a non-Christian who appears more open to spiritual things exists, why wait? If you're thinking of writing a letter to a relative to warmly explain the plan of salvation, do it now. If someone at the grocery store appears open to reading a tract that you have, why wait until the next time to give it? Give it today! If there needs to be an outreach through your church to the lost, start planning it today. If you are thinking about witnessing to a business acquaintance over lunch, schedule that lunch today. Why procrastinate?

When considering our outreach to non-Christians, we must always be mindful that we have today. We may not have tomorrow.

TIP #59

A HEALTHY PRESSURE IS THE PRESSURE TO MAKE THE GOSPEL CLEAR.

Unhealthy and Healthy Pressure

Pressure is healthy as long as it is the right kind. For example, every worker should feel the pressure of representing his firm well through both character and conduct. He is then a benefit and not a detriment to the firm. Unhealthy pressure would be the need to meet a financial goal, even if the means used are unethical. It could also be the pressure to get a signature on a contract, even though the customer feels uncertain of what he is signing.

Pressure is healthy in evangelism as long as it's the right kind. Unhealthy pressure is the need to bring a person to Christ today. People come to Christ in His timing, not ours. Equally wrong is the pressure of feeling like we must explain the gospel to a person the first time we meet them. That indeed may be the best time, but it also may be a time when you need to develop a relationship with them, which hopefully allows you to present the gospel at a later date.

One pressure in evangelism is healthy: the pressure to make the gospel clear. If a person fails to understand the gospel because of spiritual blindness that only the Holy Spirit can remove, that is not our responsibility, but we should feel the pressure to make the gospel so clear that it not only can be understood, it also cannot be misunderstood.

That means we must speak clearly to three issues. 1) We must come to God as sinners. Romans 3:23 says, "for all have sinned and fall short of the glory of God." We have missed His standard of perfection and deserve to be forever separated from Him. 2) Christ's death was a substitutionary death. Romans 5:8 tells us, "But God demonstrates His own love toward us, in that while we were still sinners, Christ died for us." He took the punishment that we deserved for our sins, died in our place, and rose on the third day. 3) The way we receive His free gift of eternal life purchased through His death and resurrection is by trusting Christ *alone* to save us. Romans 5:1 says, "Therefore, having been justified by faith, we have peace with God through our Lord Jesus Christ." Only through trusting Christ alone to save us are we justified in His sight.

Healthy pressure in evangelism is the pressure to speak clearly, not confusingly, when presenting the gospel. Lay aside the unhealthy pressure, but embrace the healthy pressure in evangelism.

TIP #60

YOU HAVE TO DISCERN WHAT KIND OF "FOOL" YOU ARE TRYING TO REACH.

To Say or Not to Say

Sometimes the Bible appears to contradict itself. It says one thing in one sentence and another in the next. After study, though, when we understand the message, we gain tremendous truth.

Proverbs 26:4–5 is a good example. "Do not answer a fool according to his folly, lest you also be like him. Answer a fool according to his folly, lest he be wise in his own eyes." One might respond, "Wow, I'm confused. What am I supposed to do?" The answer is both. The wise writer gives us a lesson everyone in evangelism needs to hear.

A non-Christian may behave and talk like a fool. He has no desire to listen. He's an impossible person with whom to reason. His mouth is in gear and his mind isn't. To talk to such a person and get him to understand spiritual matters you have to reduce yourself to his level. In a sense you are encouraging him to continue his senseless conversation. Your best witness to him may be to say nothing at that moment.

There is another kind of "fool" for which the opposite is true. He has thought through his reasons, but his reasons are faulty. Instead of saying nothing, you need to say something. Otherwise you may encourage him to think his reasoning is wise and what he says has an element of truth in it. The fact is, his words and thoughts are foolish. His reasoning is that of a person who has been untouched by the Spirit of God. As the Scriptures tell us, "But the natural man does not receive the things of the Spirit of God, for they are foolishness to him;

nor can he know them, because they are spiritually discerned" (1 Corinthians 2:14). Your words properly spoken and used by the Holy Spirit might show him the fallacy of his thinking.

How do you know the difference? The Holy Spirit gives discernment. As you seek direction from the Holy Spirit, God guides you as to what is needed. Some who are foolish in their reasoning need nothing said to them while others need to hear something. Asking God for direction and benefiting from experience helps you know what is best at that moment. You are letting the Spirit direct you as you practice obedience in evangelism.

As you witness to someone who would fit Proverbs' description of a fool, ask yourself, "What kind of fool is he? One who needs nothing said or one who needs something said?"

TIP #61

THOSE WE LEAD TO CHRIST EARLY IN THEIR LIVES HAVE TIME TO EARN ETERNAL REWARDS.

Loving and Fair

Non-Christians sometimes have a particular struggle when considering our salvation message. God seems a bit unfair. A nine-year-old person comes to Christ and receives the free gift of eternal life. A ninety-year-old person with five minutes to live comes to Christ on his deathbed. He, too, receives the free gift of eternal life. How could a ninety-year-old profit the same way a nine-year-old does?

This struggle overlooks two truths. The first has to do with the gravity of sin. That is, the nine-year-old didn't deserve eternal life any more than the ninety-year-old. Being who we are, it is a marvel that God would save any of us at any age.

The second has to do with the difference between eternal salvation and eternal rewards. The Bible speaks of the free gift of eternal life, which is available to everyone, everywhere. But the Bible also speaks of heavenly rewards, those which God gives in recognition of a life that has been lived for Him.

First Corinthians 3:12–15 reads,

Now if anyone builds on this foundation *with* gold, silver, precious stones, wood, hay, straw, each one's work will become clear; for the Day will declare it, because it will be revealed by fire; and the fire will test each one's work, of what sort it is. If anyone's work which he has built on *it* endures, he will receive a reward. If anyone's work is burned, he will suffer loss; but he himself will be saved, yet so as through fire.

The analogy of fire is fitting because in the day of the New Testament it was used to test the quality of metals. Gold, silver, and precious stones represent works that upon examination are worthy of reward. Wood, hay, and stone represent works that are not. God rewards those who faithfully follow Christ and whose works and motives honor him.

An elderly person coming to Christ on his deathbed wins and loses. He wins because he is forever with the Savior. He loses because there is no time left to live for Christ and be rewarded. A young person who comes to Christ has an entire life to live for Him and be appropriately rewarded in His presence. "Well done," will mean everything when we look into the face of the Savior.

God is loving, but He is also fair. Those who come to Him and live for Him will be rewarded. That is one of many reasons for coming to Christ sooner, not later.

TIP #62

DON'T JUST THINK OF YOUR NEIGHBOR; THINK OF YOUR NEIGHBORHOOD.

Expand Your Vision

Ever attempt to look at everything in life through God's eyes instead of yours? It will affect the way you view your friends and your enemies, your today and your tomorrow, your actions and your attitude, everything in life that goes right and everything that goes wrong.

It even affects how many you view as being in need of the gospel. Often, people come to our training seminars with a particular person they want to reach in mind—a relative back home, a supervisor at work, a tennis or racquetball partner, a parent or grown child, or perhaps their investment counselor. There's nothing wrong with that, but God's vision is much bigger. You see your friends; He sees beyond them to your friends' friends. You see your running partner; He also sees the parents of your running partner. You see your supervisor; He sees the one who supervises him. You see your neighbor; He sees your neighborhood.

That's what makes Acts 1:8 so meaningful. "But you shall receive power when the Holy Spirit has come upon you; and you shall be witnesses to Me in Jerusalem, and in all Judea and Samaria, and to the end of the earth." Christ's concern? *The whole earth!* They were to begin at Jerusalem, continue through Judea and Samaria, and keep going until they reached the uttermost parts of the earth.

Everyone needed to hear. No one was excluded from His vision. As you pray for your neighbor, take a moment from time to time to pray for his neighbor. As you pray for your friends, pause someday and pray for *their* friends.

Through prayer, God will increase your vision. You'll begin to see in a greater way than ever that not just your friends or coworkers need Him, but the entire world needs Him. You may find yourself wanting to go on a short-term mission trip or invite other Christians to join you in being trained in evangelism. After all, there are people *they* need to reach that you will never meet.

Attempt to look at life through God's eyes. You'll soon be looking at the lost through His eyes as well. Your concern is for the neighbor next door. God's concern is for the neighbor next door to him and the one next door to him, plus the one next door to him, plus . . . got it? Anyone, anywhere, everyone, everywhere.

TIP #63

VIEW YOUR NEXT OPPORTUNITY AS A PERSON, NOT A PROJECT.

Treat People Like People

Do you know what stuck out to me when I read the Bible as a new convert? Christ treated people as people—individuals who needed His help. Each one was different and each one had his own set of baggage, yet still they were people, not projects. Special categories or groups didn't seem to exist with Him. So individualized was He that when teaching a multitude, He was attracted to particular people. Note that I said attracted to, not distracted by.

For example, in Matthew 9, He's speaking with many people, but He sees a paralytic on a bed and says, "Son, be of good cheer; your sins are forgiven you" (v. 2). He sees Matthew sitting in his tax office and says, "Follow Me" (v. 9). He readily accepts an invitation to come to a ruler's house to help his daughter who was presumed dead (v. 18). En route, He heals a woman who had a hemorrhage for twelve years (v. 20). He doesn't stop there. He takes the time to heal two blind men (v. 29) and one who is demon possessed (v. 32). Jesus gave each person individualized attention. They weren't projects to Him. He didn't categorize them. He never saw the situations as another healing to do, another difficulty to solve, or another duty to fulfill. They were people with real needs, different hurts and feelings, and varying backgrounds.

That's how non-Christians whom we meet every day must be viewed—as people, not projects. All of them have varying needs, different backgrounds, assorted hurts and feelings. Often as I train believers in evangelism, they ask, "If a non-Christian said or did this (example) what would you say?" I respect the fact that they would like to learn from someone who has had extensive experience in evangelism. But each time I am faced with that question, I feel a bit frustrated. Until I have a chance to talk to that person, ask them questions, and get more information, I don't know for sure what I would say or do. Each situation varies because each person varies.

How are you viewing your next opportunity to evangelize? Is it just another obligation to meet, another presentation to make, or another outreach event in which to participate? Or do you see the loneliness of Joe, the hopelessness of Holly, Bill's marriage and family struggles? People need to be to us what they were to Jesus—people, not projects.

TIP #64

DON'T WRITE ANYONE OFF.

No One Is Unreachable

"I cannot fathom that person ever coming to Christ." "She'd be the last person in the world who'd ever be interested in spiritual things." "Even if Jesus Christ Himself were to speak to him, he wouldn't be interested." "There is absolutely no one who will ever get through to her."

Have you made one of those statements? You've seen someone so opposed to spiritual things that in your opinion, it would take a piece of spiritual dynamite to crack the callousness.

Do you know what is interesting? Years ago, someone may have said the same thing about you. If God could get through to you, He can certainly get through to them. Why give up on them when God did not give up on you?

One of the best examples of the depth of God's reach is the apostle Paul. He did everything he could to stamp out Christianity. He encouraged the killing of as many as possible. He watched and cheered as believers were stoned to death. But on the road to Damascus everything changed. In the matter of a moment he went from fighting God to following Him (see Acts 9).

Now listen to his testimony as he explains it to his young assistant Timothy. He says,

This is a faithful saying and worthy of all acceptance, that Christ Jesus came into the world to save sinners, of whom I am chief. However, for this reason I obtained mercy, that in me first Jesus Christ might show all long-suffering, as a pattern to those who are going to believe on Him for everlasting life. (1 Timothy 1:15–16)

Paul referred to himself as the top sinner, but he testifies that his own salvation had a God-ordained purpose behind it. He calls himself a "pattern." *Pattern* should be considered as an example, sketch, or illustration. I believe that one of the reasons God saved Paul was to prove He could save anyone. Paul's testimony shouts to anyone anywhere, "If God can save me, He can save you."

Whenever you struggle with doubting whether or not someone is going to come to Christ, allow Paul's testimony to shout, "Look what He did with me." God didn't give up on Paul. He didn't give up on you, and neither has He given up on your non-Christian friend. No one is outside of His love. No one is outside of His reach. The person deemed unreachable by you is not unreachable by Him.

TIP #65

THE PAINFUL EXPERIENCE OF DEATH CAN OPEN UP OPPORTUNITIES FOR THE GOSPEL.

The Joyful Side of a Painful Experience

There are some subjects that Christians and non-Christians alike don't enjoy talking about. But the Christian has a distinct advantage in some of them.

Death is one of those subjects. Death is what I call a delightfully painful subject to talk about. Painful because we don't always know the means through which death will be experienced. A friend of mine who died of acute leukemia several years ago said, "I want to go to heaven, but the process is painful." Mercifully, as with others I know, God shortened the process to make it less painful. At the same time it is delightful because there is not a Christian alive who should not look forward to seeing Jesus face-to-face.

Death's reality can be an effective foundation to talk to non-Christians. Isaiah 25:8 is a great verse to use. We read,

He will swallow up death forever,
and the Lord God will wipe away tears from all faces;
The rebuke of His people
He will take away from all the earth;
For the Lord has spoken.

Scriptures do not deny the dread of death. Isaiah used the words, "He will swallow up death forever." Death is seen at times in the Scriptures as a large mouth that consumes people—not exactly a pleasant thought. But this dread is a temporary phenomenon. Death is only experienced once, and one day it will no longer exist (1 Corinthians 15:54–55). In heaven an all-powerful and sovereign God will have extinguished it. So much so that Isaiah tells us, "The Lord God will wipe away tears from all faces." In heaven, dying is over. It's a thing of the past. How can we be certain of that? Isaiah concludes the verse by saying, "For the Lord has spoken." God means what He says. The certainty of no more death is as sure as the very word of God.

What a cause to celebrate! What a guarantee! What a victory! Although painful, when it is over, it is over. Done, gone, past, forever behind us. We are forever in His presence.

Don't avoid a subject many people find difficult to talk about. Just explain why one can be both relieved and excited at the thought of death. God brings comfort and even joy in the midst of the pain. We can be personally related to the One who "swallowed up" death and wipes away all tears. What a great reason to know Him.

TIP #66

PRAY THAT GOD WILL BRING SOMEONE ELSE TO HELP REACH FAMILY.

Family Can Be Tough

People can be hard to reach. Some of the hardest ones are those in your own family.

The reasons are numerous: Closeness may cause your unbelieving relatives to hear but not listen. Your voice is sometimes too familiar. Family members who don't know the Lord can't accept your newfound faith. The latter is particularly true when children try to reach their non-Christian parents. It's hard for them to accept the fact that you may know something that they don't. Then there is the problem that they know you too well. Your past behavior is an excuse that Satan uses with lightning speed. "We knew you when . . ." Furthermore, some families don't communicate about anything they consider private. Sex, money, and spiritual matters top the list.

Christ predicted this. He experienced it in His own family (John 7:5). As He spoke of discipleship, He warned, "'And a man's enemies will be those of his own household'" (Matthew 10:36). The Bible says that all people take a stand on the person of Christ (John 3:18). If you have not trusted Christ, you have rejected Him. Our beliefs about who Christ is divides people. You are either His child or not His child. You are either saved or lost. This is especially painful in a family when you have a shared past but now have a divided future.

You may need to pray for an assistant—someone who is not a member of the family. As you pray for laborers in evangelism (Luke 10:2), ask God to send someone in *addition* to you to speak to them. The kingdom of heaven will be filled with people who were led to Christ by someone outside the family. That "someone's" biggest advantage is just that: she is outside the family.

You may feel the burden of being the only Christian in the lives of your family. Your family may have no contact with Christians. They may not go to church. Or they may have had negative experiences with Christians in the past. All the more reason to pray for another laborer! God can penetrate any defense Satan creates. God can bring just the right person across their path and make that eternal difference.

Do everything you can to reach your family. Remember that that includes praying for someone who can come alongside you to speak to those you love but find difficult to reach.

TIP #67

HARD TIMES ARE OFTEN GREAT TIMES FOR THE GOSPEL.

Hard Times Have Advantages

Worried? Scared? Confused? Disillusioned? Depressed? Hard times often incite burdensome emotions. But these times can be particularly difficult for those who don't know the Lord. Whether because of personal hardships, terrorism, the economy, natural disasters, or tragedies that grip the nation's attention, unbelievers are afraid of both today and tomorrow.

Questions instantly come to their mind. Do I move to a remote part of the nation where nobody knows where I am? Do I try to get a second job as backup should I lose the one I have? Where do I put my investments, and is anything safe? Do I just surrender to all the forces and let happen what may? What will my family do if the diagnosis is cancer?

This is when we have a powerful message to give to the lost—God is in control. For the Christian, we have nothing to fear because of Romans 8:28. There we read, "And we know that all things work together for good to those who love God, to those who are called according to His purpose." As a song says, "I know who holds tomorrow and I know who holds my hand" ("I Know Who Holds Tomorrow," Ira Stanphill).

But to convey that message, we need to get to the heart of the gospel. They don't need to know *about* the God that is in control. They need to *know* the God that is in control. It's a relationship with Him that brings security. We are His now and we are His forever. That means we need to explain that all of us are sinners, and that Christ died for us, took the punishment for our sins, and rose again. We need to trust in Him alone as our only way to eternal life. Once we do, we are instantly His children. The Bible tells us, "But as many as received Him, to them He gave the right to become children of God, to those who believe on His name" (John 1:12). Circumstances may get worse, but when everything is out of control, He is in control and we are eternally His.

Hard times can sometimes offer better opportunities for the gospel than good times. Good times can dull people to their need of the Lord (Deuteronomy 6:1–12). Our language and our lives have to send the same clear message: if we know Him, there is no need to fear today or tomorrow.

TIP #68

CURRENT EVENTS ILLUSTRATE BIBLICAL TRUTH.

And Now the News

As one evangelizes, it's helpful to keep two things within one's grip—the Bible and the evening news. The Bible, of course, is the most important. It establishes the message we have for lost people. But the evening news also helps. Current events confirm the truth of the Bible. They show the lost our need for a Savior.

Jesus, the master communicator, set the example. In Luke 13:1–5, He told of two tragic events that made front-page news. One event concerned people who came to Galilee for one of the feasts and were then killed at the hands of Pilate. The other concerned a tragic fall of a tower that killed eighteen people. Christ's point was that neither event happened because the victims were greater sinners. Unless His listeners repented they too would perish. In context, by "perish" Jesus is probably referring to the fall of Jerusalem, not to an eternal hell. Jesus used current events to explain the Bible's message that we are all sinners in need of Him.

Almost every day events occur in the news that illustrate the truth of Scripture. These events may surround the violence of the human heart or the depravity of man. A mass killing, the hatred a person has for another, the selfishness of ones who robbed homes and businesses that were devastated by a tornado—all show the wickedness of the human heart. Imagine people wanting to profit from the unavoidable misfortune of others. They verify what the Bible says, "The heart is deceitful above all things, and desperately wicked" (Jeremiah 17:9).

Every day we see the futility people experience as they search for happiness and meaning in life, such as the executive who commits suicide and leaves a note to explain that he is giving up his search. We can show the lost that the Bible says happiness doesn't come from having something but from knowing Someone. Christ said, "I have come that they may have life, and that they may have it more abundantly" (John 10:10).

Still other current events speak of the brevity of life—one who suddenly dies of cancer only diagnosed a month earlier or the tragic death of a twenty-year-old who had a heart ailment he never knew about. They illustrate what James 4:13–14 emphasizes: life is like a vapor, here today, gone tomorrow. The time to come to Christ is now.

Walk in Christ's footsteps. Keep the message of the gospel your priority, but know how to illustrate it through current events.

TIP #69

PREPARE YOURSELF FOR MIXED RESPONSES IN EVANGELISM.

Not Everyone Responds the Same

On almost any subject, people disagree—education, politics, investments, child-rearing, and a host of other items. People have differing ideas. That is most certainly true when it comes to spiritual matters. Whether it is over the person of Christ, the trustworthiness of the Bible, or the reality of the hereafter, people disagree. That is one reason that we should not be surprised in receiving mixed reactions to our message as we evangelize. It happened in the day of the New Testament, and it happens today.

In Acts 17, Paul is brought to the Areopagus, otherwise called Mars Hill, where the political leaders of the city met to discuss the latest ideas. Mars Hill was the place to go to understand all matters of religion and morality. Paul was brought there because he had "preached to them Jesus and the resurrection" (Acts 17:18). The leaders questioned, "May we know what this new doctrine is of which you speak?" (Acts 17:19). So what was the response? The same thing that happens almost every time the gospel is preached. Acts 17:32–34 explains,

> And when they heard of the resurrection of the dead, some mocked, while others said, "We will hear you again on this matter." So Paul departed from among them. However, some men joined him and believed, among them Dionysius the Areopagite, a woman named Damaris, and others with them.

Some must have thought the message or even the messenger was a joke. They had no desire to hear more. Others said, "Let's talk some more." Their interest was aroused. Still others believed. It's interesting that one of those who believed was Dionysius, a member of the political council.

Having the right expectations as we evangelize can be a great help. Expecting a variety of responses can make us better prepared to receive them. It prevents us from setting ourselves up for disappointment or having unrealistic expectations. We should hope that all of those we evangelize will come to Christ, but we also have to be realistic in realizing that not all will. Because of where they are and to what degree the Holy Spirit has softened their hearts, there will be differing responses. We can expect to meet everyone from those who have little or no concern for spiritual matters to those who are prepared to trust the Savior.

A declaration or discussion of spiritual matters brings mixed responses. Expect them and you will prepare yourself emotionally and spiritually for them.

SPEAK THE TRUTH
IN LOVE

TIP #70

LOOKING FROM THE PERSON TO THE PROBLEM WILL MAKE YOU MORE COMPASSIONATE.

Through a Different Lens

Have you ever noticed how irritating some non-Christians can be? Self-centered. Arrogant. Rude. Uncaring. Stubborn. Self-righteous. Just like a few Christians I know!

Perhaps that's one reason why believers sometimes don't enjoy being around unbelievers. My response is twofold. For one, any Christians living for Christ should be more enjoyable to be around than unbelievers. Second, it's very interesting that the Bible never emphasizes, "Do you enjoy non-Christians?" Instead it asks, "Do you have compassion for them?"

Take one of my favorite verses, Matthew 9:36. We read, "But when He saw the multitudes, He was moved with compassion for them, because they were weary and scattered, like sheep having no shepherd." "Compassion" means to have pity or feel sympathy toward someone.

Why was He compassionate toward them? It was because of their *condition*—they were "like sheep having no shepherd." Ephesians 2:1 describes our condition prior to coming to Christ. It says, "And you He made alive, who were *dead in trespasses and sins*" (italics mine). We often see what people do. Christ sees who they are—people without Him.

That's why it is important not to see lost people through your eyes. If you do, you will focus on the hurtful and harmful things they do, things that cause wounds (emotionally or even physically) to themselves or others. But if you focus on who they are, you deal with the cause, not the symptom. Non-Christians act and do the things they do because of the sinful condition they are in as people without a relationship with Christ. After all, they are untouched by the spirit of God. They are "dead in trespasses and sins."

When you see them through Christ's eyes, you recognize that before there can be a change on the outside, there has to be a change on the inside. The message you have for them is life transforming. Seeing them through Christ's eyes even increases the urgency to talk to them. Another day having not received that message is another day of purposeless, unfulfilled, sinful living. They need to hear about Christ and need to hear about Him *now*. Only the message of the gospel can make dead people alive.

Seeing people through your eyes results in irritation. Seeing them through Christ's eyes results in an invitation to come to the One whose specialty is making miracles out of messes. Whose eyes are you viewing unbelievers through, yours or His?

TIP #71

TRUTH MUST BE ACCOMPANIED BY GRACE, AND GRACE MUST BE ACCOMPANIED BY TRUTH.

Christ-Like Balance Is Critical

Have you ever noticed that some people don't seem to know what T-A-C-T means? They sometimes pride themselves on being "in your face." They have truth but little grace.

Others are so tactful they never confront people with their need for Christ. It appears all they desire to do is build a friendship. The brevity of life is of little consideration. They are polite to a fault. They have grace but are afraid to confront people with the truth.

The answer is contained in two words—Christlike balance. In any conversation truth and grace must come with balance. No one in the entire Bible demonstrates a balance between those two approaches better than Christ Himself. In a conversation with an unbeliever He could practice tender directness.

Take the example of the Samaritan woman of John 8, a woman caught in the very act of adultery, an act punishable by stoning. The scribes and Pharisees brought the woman to Jesus and publicly asked him, "Teacher, this woman was caught in adultery, in the very act. Now Moses, in the law, commanded us that such should be stoned. But what do You say?" (vv. 3–5).

How did Christ demonstrate truth? He never denied her sin. He called her sin what it was—sin. "He who is without sin among you, let him throw a stone at her first" (v. 7). He never denied that she had sinned.

How did He demonstrate grace? He pointed out to her that the only one with a right to condemn her was the one with a passionate desire to save her. "Neither do I condemn you; go and sin no more," He said (v. 11). While the Pharisees were only interested in sentencing her, Christ wanted to save her. She experienced truth and grace from the One she most needed.

It is that Christlike balance we all need. The non-Christian needs to know we are all sinners and without Christ, we are facing an eternal hell. To soften that message is dishonoring to God. They also, however, need to know that we genuinely care for them and want the very best for them—life with Christ.

Pray a simple prayer as you evangelize—God give me a Christlike balance. If you have truth filled with grace and grace filled with truth you have the tender directness that honors Christ.

TIP #72

MANIPULATION IN EVANGELISM IS NEITHER RIGHT NOR NECESSARY.

There Is No Place for It

"Buy one, get one free." What the store failed to disclose is that over the last month prices were increased almost one hundred percent.

"No obligation." What isn't disclosed is that your name will be put in a database for circulation nationwide.

We've become accustomed to manipulative techniques in the world. Such techniques have infiltrated every area of the marketplace. Unfortunately, manipulation too often exists in evangelism. A Christian invites a non-Christian to an evangelistic event without revealing the content of the program, and the unbeliever is surprised to discover the event's religious nature. Or a believer approaches an unbeliever about spiritual things out of sincere concern, but since the unbeliever is a person of means, all of a sudden the conversation turns to how his finances would be of help to the church's building program.

Manipulation has two problems. One, it is dishonoring to God. God is honored by truth and sincerity, not manipulation. We should be able to say what Paul the apostle said,

> For our boasting is this: the testimony of our conscience that we conducted ourselves in the world in simplicity and godly sincerity, not with fleshly wisdom but by the grace of God, and more abundantly toward you. (2 Corinthians 1:12)

When the Corinthians accused Paul of a lack of sincerity, his integrity and humility affirmed otherwise. His priorities and practices spoke for themselves.

Second, manipulation is not necessary. The message is powerful enough to bring any unbeliever to Christ. In Romans 1:16 Paul testified, "For I am not ashamed of the gospel of Christ, for it is the power of God to salvation for everyone who believes, for the Jew first and also for the Greek." Paul had experienced this. In his own life, the gospel transformed him within a moment from one who persecuted Christians to one who emulated Christ.

Anyone in evangelism can tell you of that power. They've seen it firsthand. A man walks into an evangelistic event a convinced atheist and walks out a new Christian. A woman has no desire to meet Jesus, but as her friend shares the simplicity of the gospel, tears well up in the woman's eyes and she comes to Christ. A drug addict comes to Christ and no longer needs needles or pills.

God uses the message, not manipulation. Turn the message loose. Share it clearly, and witness its power. It can turn the most callous sinner into a committed Christian. No manipulation needed.

TIP #73

PERSONAL LETTERS EXPLAINING THE GOSPEL CAN BE EXTREMELY EFFECTIVE.

Three Powerful Tools at Your Fingertips

After many frustrating conversations, one believer wrote a letter to her unbelieving father to share her heart and the gospel with him. He never responded. Years later, sick in bed with cancer, he trusted Christ. He died two weeks later. Going through his things after the funeral, the woman found the letter she'd written to her father, opened, creased, and soft as cotton. That letter in which she shared the gospel had its impact.

God wrote the first gospel-sharing letter. The fourth book in the New Testament, John, is a letter telling us how to receive eternal life. John 20:30–31 tells us,

> And truly Jesus did many other signs in the presence of His disciples, which are not written in this book; but these are written that you may believe that Jesus is the Christ, the Son of God, and that believing you may have life in His name.

What makes letters so effective? The same thing that in many ways makes the gospel of John effective.

First, John was written by someone who cared enough for you to write an entire letter addressing your eternal destiny. In the book of John, God wrote through the author, John. With your letter, God writes through you. Any unbeliever knows it took time and concern on your part to write such a letter. It's even truer in a day when emailing or texting takes less time and effort.

Second, while a conversation goes in one ear and out the other, a letter can be read and reread. There have been times when the unbeliever did not even acknowledge receiving the letter, but kept reading and rereading it. Only eternity will reveal how many have come to Christ through the reading of the gospel of John. Only eternity will reveal the part your letters to loved ones played in bringing them to Christ.

Any letter should make the gospel as clear as John does. One cannot read the gospel of John without being struck by the fact that 1) we are sinners, 2) Christ died for us, rose again, and ascended into heaven, and 3) we have to trust Christ alone to save us. Your letter should be just as clear.

While you can't claim to have written letters divinely inspired without error as the gospel of John is (2 Timothy 3:16–17), as you are moved by the Holy Spirit, a pen, paper, and an envelope can be divinely used to change a person's eternal destiny. These are three powerful tools that are not only instruments in *your* hands, but they are also instruments in *His* hands.

TIP #74

BE CAREFUL OF THE TERMINOLOGY YOU USE WHEN INVITING PEOPLE TO COME TO CHRIST.

Choose Your Words Carefully

Have you ever had someone give you instructions that you totally misunderstood? In sorting out the confusion, he may have explained, "I know that's what I said, but that's not what I meant." The problem is you couldn't read his mind; you could only listen to his words. Incorrect terminology can be confusing.

Nowhere should that be of greater concern than evangelism. Evangelistic presentations often err on what they ask unbelievers to do. They often clearly explain that we are sinners and Christ died for us as our substitute and rose again. But when explaining what the non-Christian needs to do, the terminology becomes very confusing.

"Invite Jesus into your heart."

"Give your life to God."

"Take Him now as your Savior."

"Give your heart to Jesus."

"Say yes to Christ right now."

Why are they confusing? When a person, especially a child, hears, "Invite him into your heart" or "Give your heart to Jesus," they may think of a literal heart. How do I give Him the fleshly organ I need to live? People who hear, "Give your life to God," may doubt the effectiveness of their salvation since so many temptations grip them every day. They don't understand that the surrender of a life is part of discipleship, not salvation. If I'm encouraged to "Take Him as my Savior" or "Say yes to Christ right now," how do I do that? By going to church, being baptized, or trying to live differently?

What does the Bible tell an unbeliever to do? Christ's clear and unmistakable words were, "He who believes in Him is not condemned; but he who does not believe is condemned already, because he has not believed in the name of the only begotten Son of God" (John 3:18). *Believe* has the idea of reliance upon, dependence upon, and trust. In fact, no word explains *believe* better than the word *trust*. We come to Him as sinners, recognize Christ died on the cross in our place and rose again, and trust in Christ alone to save us. Our belief and attitude of heart is, "If He cannot get me to heaven, I'm going to hell. He and He alone can pardon and save me because He paid the price of my sin in full."

So when inviting an unbeliever to come to Christ, a great question is, "Is there anything keeping you from *trusting* Christ right now?" Correct terminology clarifies.

A person's eternal destiny is at stake. Speak language that clarifies, not language that confuses.

TIP #75

USE "WE" MORE THAN "YOU" AS MUCH AS POSSIBLE.

Include Yourself

What are the criticisms unbelievers have of Christians? One that often arises is that Christians are hypocrites. Sometimes that is an unfair accusation, because we are not and cannot be perfect. Other times, it is a proper accusation because we are not even trying to live the life we profess.

There is another that often comes up. Unbelievers often say, "Christians are arrogant." Then in explaining what they mean, they cite the fact that Christians act like they alone know the secret to living forever.

We cannot apologize for that assertion. Of course we act like we know the secret. We do! God made us a promise He cannot break. In 1 John 5:13, we are told, "These things I have written to you who believe in the name of the Son of God, that you may know that you have eternal life." The fact that we have eternal life through trusting Christ alone to save us is a "know so" not a "hope so."

There is a way, though, we can help non-Christians who struggle with the perception that Christians are arrogant. Instead of using *you*, we should be abundant in our use of *we*. *We* has a way of communicating humility, not arrogance.

In explaining our sinfulness before God, to use "you are a sinner" could be perceived as self-righteous. A non-Christian might think, "In other words, I'm a sinner but you are not." But when we explain, "We are sinners," they know that you are in the same predicament they are.

In the Old Testament, Isaiah is a good example. He was a tremendous prophet to his nation, but what does he say as he is used by God to pen the words of Scripture? In Isaiah 53:6

he said, "All we like sheep have gone astray; we have turned, every one, to his own way; and the Lord has laid on Him the iniquity of us all" (Isaiah 53:6).

At each step of a gospel presentation, *we* language becomes more effective than *you*. Because *we* all have sinned, *we* have earned death. Christ died for *us*. *We* have to trust Christ to save *us*.

It is important in evangelism to show you're not someone apart from them, but you are one of them. The use of *we* begins to tear down any thoughts they may have that you are prideful.

Yes, we know we have eternal life, but it is all because God saves sinners. *We* are all sinners.

TIP #76

PEOPLE WHO WORRY ABOUT OFFENDING OTHERS ARE NOT THE ONES WHO DO.

Who Offends and Who Doesn't

One of the fears about evangelism believers often express is the fear of offending someone. To these believers, I often say, "Don't worry about it." Why would I say such a thing? I've found that the people who express that concern are the very people who usually never offend. The fact that they express that concern demonstrates their care and sensitivity. They desire to find a loving attitude and the proper words to approach someone. I have often asked those people, "Can you give me one example of someone you offended?" I cannot recall any such person giving me an example.

In contrast, those who offend don't express such concern. They simply offend and sometimes defend their insensitive approach by saying, "Well, I told them the truth. I can't help it if they don't like it." If you tend to be like that, it would be helpful to consider what you want to communicate to the unbeliever and how you can say it in a way that demonstrates care. When you were an unbeliever, is that how you would have wanted him to approach you?

Secondly, let's step back and ask, "What is my responsibility?" It is summed up in a few words. Ephesians 4:15 says, ". . . speaking the truth in love. . ." The meaning is unmistakable. Everything that comes from the mouth of a believer should be honest and true and should always be said in a loving manner. Truth affects what we say and love affects how we say it. To God, both the truth and how it is spoken matters.

When words are spoken in that manner, often the person is not offended. He knows what you are telling him is not necessarily what he wants to hear, but you are convinced he needs to hear it. Even if at the moment a person seems perturbed as he thinks about the conversation you had with him, he often ultimately concludes that you meant it for his best. If he *is* offended, you cannot and need not apologize (you might express regret that he is offended without apologizing for sharing the truth). You have done what God called you to do. The person's reaction is not your responsibility.

Take heart from the fact that if one of your first concerns is that you don't offend, that is a good thing. It demonstrates that you pay careful attention to both what you say and how you say it. So go share the gospel.

TIP #77

SAYING, "I'M SORRY" WHEN EVANGELIZING CAN ENHANCE YOUR WITNESS TO UNBELIEVERS.

Pause to Apologize

It's been said that the one phrase not used enough in our relationships is, "I'm sorry." Let's talk about those two words. Husbands, wives, and children who are believers are encouraged to practice apologizing toward those they've offended within their home or within their church. We're taught the biblical principle of speaking *to* one another, not *about* one another, when we've been offended (James 5:16). Too often though, we fail to realize the need to say "I'm sorry" with those offenses we've committed before unbelievers.

Hebrews 12:14 contains a strong admonition. The problem is we miss a three-letter word when we read it. The text says, "Pursue peace with all people, and holiness, without which no one will see the Lord." The three-letter word we often overlook is "all" people. The writer of Hebrews instructs us to pursue peace with everyone, not simply believers.

Accompanying the pursuit of peace should be the pursuit of holiness. What better way to pursue peace and practice holiness than to say, "I'm sorry" when we've offended unbelievers?

Don't misunderstand the phrase, "without which no one will see the Lord." Proper actions toward unbelievers will not earn us eternal life. There are two ways of understanding the last part of that verse in keeping with the context. First, when believers are in God's presence they will be as holy as He is holy (1 John 3:2). Second, those who seek to live pure and holy lives are the ones who have the best perception and understanding of God's will, His ways, and His works. Either way, "I'm sorry" is one of the ways we pursue peace with all men and practice holiness before the Lord. Yes, we wronged them, but "I'm sorry" reduces rather than enhances conflict and demonstrates that we are godly enough to ask for forgiveness. Godliness is seen in the humility and honesty that resulted in "I'm sorry."

Have you lost your temper with a non-Christian who hurt your feelings? He may not be justified in what he did, but neither are you justified in how you responded. Don't wait for his apology; give him yours. Is an unbeliever annoyed by your hypocrisy in an area you've confessed but never changed? "I'm sorry" may cause him to ponder that if you can recognize your wrongs before him, can he not recognize his wrongs before God?

You would be hard-pressed to find one instance where "I'm sorry" has hurt one's relationship with a non-Christian. You could find many places it has helped.

TIP #78

WHEN IT'S APPROPRIATE, DON'T HESITATE TO ASK THE CLOSING QUESTION.

Be a Closer

An insurance agent I know was surprised when a friend of his bought a life insurance policy from a stranger instead of him. He approached the friend and asked, "Why didn't you buy it from me?" The friend answered, "You never asked me to."

One reason many Christians have not had the opportunity of actually leading someone to Christ is that they have not *asked* anyone to trust Christ. They've presented the gospel but have stopped short of saying, "Is there anything keeping you from trusting Christ right now?" They open the conversations but hesitate to close them.

There are certainly times when asking such a closing question is not appropriate. A person who has just heard the good news may need a bit of time to think about it. There are other times the person is so ripe for the gospel that the time to ask him to trust Christ is now. Why wait? The people of Samaria were a good example. Because they were prepared spiritually for the gospel through the Old Testament prophets or the ministry of John the Baptist, they were receptive of the gospel message. John 4:39 says, "And many of the Samaritans of that city believed in Him because of the word of the woman who testified, 'He told me all that I ever did.'" In that story, Christ reminds us, "Do you not say, 'There are still four months and then comes the harvest'? Behold, I say to you, lift up your eyes and look at the fields, for they are already white for harvest!" (John 4:35). Four verses later we read, "And many of the Samaritans of that city believed in Him because of the word of the woman who testified, 'He told me all that I ever did'" (John 4:39).

One reason we may not ask that final question is that we fear that the unbeliever may raise objections we aren't prepared to answer. You will be pleasantly surprised at how many unbelievers are ready to settle the matter then and there as they explain, "I have just never understood it before now."

Asking is so important because a person is not saved when they clearly understand the gospel. They are saved when, upon understanding the offer of eternal life, they in faith *accept it*. Knowing how to be saved means they know about God. Trusting Christ means they now know God. They don't merely know about His offer of eternal life; they've actually received it.

The point is to ask. Don't deny yourself the privilege of leading someone to the Savior by a simple failure to ask.

CONCENTRATE ON BEING FAITHFUL

TIP #79

HAVING THE RIGHT PERSPECTIVE WILL KEEP YOUR BEHAVIOR PROPER IN RESPONDING TO UNBELIEVERS.

It's Your Savior, Not Your Circumstances

Working with non-Christians is not always a pleasant experience. Untouched by the Spirit of God, they can be nasty, insulting, prideful, accusatory, self-righteous. The list goes on. It's easy to respond with the same kind of behavior. But whereas a non-Christian is controlled by the evil one, a growing believer has the Holy Spirit's help to keep those areas in check.

So what is the answer to keeping those behaviors in check as we evangelize? In one sentence, remember we have a Redeemer. That means Christ has already guaranteed that our story will end right. Here is how Proverbs 24:15–16 puts it: "Do not lie in wait, O wicked man, against the dwelling of the righteous; do not plunder his resting place; For a righteous man may fall seven times and rise again, but the wicked shall fall by calamity." I love that phrase, "For a righteous man may fall seven times and rise again." Simply put, the wicked fall never to rise; the righteous rise never to forever fall. Whatever is suffered, the righteous rise again and ultimately live forever. The wicked will never ultimately win; the righteous will never ultimately lose. We can respond to an ungracious unbeliever with grace now because we know we will be justified in the end.

But note, it's not because of who we are that we ultimately succeed. It's because of who He is. Proverbs 23:10–11 says, "Do not remove the ancient landmark, nor enter the fields of the fatherless; for their Redeemer is mighty; He will plead their cause against you." The righteous have a Redeemer, and *He* sets everything right.

So what will focusing on such eternal truth do in terms of our evangelism? Everything! For one, it keeps us from growing hateful, vengeful, bitter, frustrated, and angry. Instead it makes us sorrowful for non-Christians and inwardly grateful that we know the Savior. It actually enhances our feelings of intimacy with Him because He knows and through Him we know something that the wicked will never understand. They fall to never rise; we fall to ultimately rise again. The deeper our understanding of this truth, the greater our burden to introduce them to the Savior.

Every step we take in evangelism, regardless of what we face, ultimately ends in victory. No need to fear or get frustrated by that which can never overcome us. When we fall, get abused, or suffer anything we may in evangelism, we can dust off the damage and move on. We have a Redeemer.

TIP #80

SOMETIMES THE PROBLEM IS NOT YOUR PRESENTATION, BUT THEIR UNBELIEF.

Stop Beating Yourself Up

I consider Matthew 13:58 one of the most encouraging verses in evangelism: "Now He did not do many mighty works there because of their unbelief." You might be wondering how I consider that encouraging.

Examine the context. Jesus was in His hometown of Nazareth. In His second visit, their familiarity with Him became a problem. Jesus performed miracles to prove that He was who He said that He was, but the people were so blinded by unbelief that even miracles were not convincing to them. As He stated, "A prophet is not without honor except in his own country and in his own house" (v. 57). Their unbelief stood in the way of witnessing His power among them.

So what's the point? Their failure to believe had nothing to do with Him. It had everything to do with *them*. Though the facts were there, the people simply would not believe.

Many I've met are convinced they've done something wrong if they cannot convince someone of a particular truth about Christ. They feel that if they had chosen different words or simply presented them better, the person may have come to faith. It's so easy to ask, "What did I do wrong?"

Perhaps nothing. The other person's unbelief may be the problem. It's not that they can't believe; it's that they *won't* believe. Nothing one says or does will convince them. Only when the convicting work of the Holy Spirit breaks through will they believe.

Satan has many tactics. One of them is to get you to beat yourself up. There will always be days when you could have explained the plan of salvation better or more clearly. Don't hesitate to examine what you may have said or done differently, but please be careful how far you carry that. Jesus did everything right in every area, including evangelism. He was the perfect Son of God, yet even still some would not believe.

You, too, may have done everything right in your conversations with a few particular non-Christians. It is their unbelief that is the problem. The problem may have had nothing to do with you but everything to do with them. Continue to pray for them and witness again as God provides the opportunity. Don't let self-examination lead to self-condemnation. Self-examination in evangelism for the right reasons is helpful. Self-condemnation for any reason is destructive.

TIP #81

IT TAKES PATIENCE AND LONG-SUFFERING IN WORKING WITH NON-CHRISTIANS.

You'll Need Both

Ever examine the difference between patience and long-suffering? Patience is predominantly used in Scripture in reference to how we need to respond to difficult *situations*. It means the ability to stand up under difficulty without becoming angry or bitter. James wrote to the people scattered throughout the Roman Empire during a time of persecution. He told them, "My brethren, count it all joy when you fall into various trials, knowing that the testing of your faith produces patience. But let patience have its perfect work, that you may be perfect and complete, lacking nothing" (James 1:2–4).

Long-suffering is predominately used of the way we respond to difficult *people*. It means to stand up under the abuse of others without seeking revenge. Paul the apostle mentioned it as one of the garments believers should wear. "Therefore, as the elect of God, holy and beloved, put on tender mercies, kindness, humility, meekness, long-suffering; bearing with one another and forgiving one another" (Colossians 3:12–13).

To exercise both we must rely on His strength, not ours. Paul told the Colossians that they could be "strengthened with all might, according to His glorious power, for all patience and long-suffering with joy" (Colossians 1:11). Patience and long-suffering, the abilities to stand up under difficult situations and people, are both needed in working with non-Christians (and I might add difficult Christians, too). After all, non-Christians are untouched by the spirit of God and do the things unbelievers do.

A non-Christian has listened to you present the gospel on numerous occasions and yet shows no more interest than the first time you spoke to him. A relative misrepresents a situation you were both in and makes you the culprit when it was entirely his fault. A boss at the office takes advantage of your good work ethic and gives you a load that is unreasonable. A neighbor has stolen from you. You have proof that would stand up in a court of law. As you pray, you sense now is not the time to confront him about it. A longtime acquaintance given to alcohol addiction threatens you during one of his out-of-control moments.

God-given patience and long-suffering helps you respond properly. Keep in mind, though, that God exercised the same toward us in our lost condition and still does. All He's asking is that we extend the same patience and long-suffering toward others that He extended to us. It may not be easy, but it could be eternally rewarding.

TIP #82

LEARN FROM ANY AND ALL MISTAKES YOU HAVE MADE.

Everybody Makes Mistakes

Mistakes have a tremendous advantage. God uses them to teach us. The question we need to ask ourselves is, "Am I a victor or a victim of my mistakes?" In other words, have we mastered them or have they mastered us?

I am comforted and thrilled that when Christ invites us to follow Him as His disciples, He uses one little but meaningful word—learn. In Matthew 11:29 He said, "Take My yoke upon you and *learn* from Me" (emphasis mine). "Yoke" referred to a wooden frame placed upon one's shoulders that made a load easier to bear. In this context He is referring to His instructions on how to live a life honoring to God. Among the many things He wants to teach us is how to glorify God by introducing Jesus to others. Mistakes are one of the things He uses. To benefit from what He wants to teach us, we need to master our mistakes not let them master us.

I've been in evangelism for more than forty years. I could fill your day by telling you about the mistakes I've made. In one instance, I moved too fast in leading a person to a decision I'm not sure he was ready to make. Another time, I talked too much and listened too little. As a result I didn't pick up on something critical the person said that was the *real* problem. On still another occasion, my body language made the person feel pressure to come to Christ—pressure I did not mean to convey, nor did I realize he was feeling.

Do I regret those mistakes? Most definitely. Do I dwell on them? Absolutely not. Have I learned from them? Have I ever! The reason is rather simple. As I grew spiritually I realized that God used those mistakes to teach me. They were not a total loss. Valuable lessons were learned. I have mastered them, but I refuse to let them master me. To complete the metaphorical picture, the classroom through which He taught me those lessons was then simply labelled, "Mistakes."

God did not produce your mistakes; you did. After all, God uses imperfect people to introduce unbelievers to a perfect Savior. He wants us to be faithful; He is not expecting us to be flawless. But God wants to make you the victor, not the victim of your errors. Celebrate what you have learned from God, who uses our mistakes to teach us.

TIP #83

ALWAYS MAKE YOUR GOAL APPROVAL FROM GOD, NOT MEN.

Whose Approval Matters

Approval can be a good thing, as long as you seek it from the right person. Seeking it from the wrong person could hinder your involvement in evangelism or even cloud the message you have for the lost.

Suppose you seek to witness to a non-Christian relative who highly respects you. That relative also takes pride in his good deeds and church attendance and assumes those will get him into heaven. He becomes annoyed when someone speaks with him about the need of a personal relationship with Christ. Not wanting to lose his respect could make you hesitate to confront him with the truth of the gospel and his lost condition. It could cause you to water down the gospel to be a more palatable message to him.

A friend has stuck by you through good times and hard times, and you've stuck by him. But you've never discussed spiritual matters. Frankly, his need of Christ is something that should have been addressed years ago. To bring up the matter now, regardless of how tactfully it is done, could make him feel you are no longer his friend. After all, friends don't discuss divisive issues, do they? Instead of saying something, you say nothing, concerned that you would lose your approval from him.

Answer? Seek approval, but seek it with the only person who really matters—Jesus Christ. Let Galatians 1:10 be a verse you master, not just memorize. Paul said, "For do I now persuade men, or God? Or do I seek to please men? For if I still pleased men, I would not be a bondservant of Christ."

Paul was concerned for the purity of the gospel in the church of Galatia. There were those who, in attempting to win the acceptance of the legalizers (an influential group in the church who were adding to the gospel of grace), taught a salvation message of Christ plus, not Christ period. Paul argued that such an addition resulted in a totally different gospel, one apart from grace. Anyone who distorted the gospel of grace was deserving of God's discipline (Galatians 1:8–9). Paul was more concerned about God's approval than the approval of a group of people.

The goal must always be to please God, not men. Approval matters greatly, as long as we seek approval from Christ. It will help us tell people what they need to hear. It will also help us keep the gospel as pure and clear as God made it. Their approval could not matter any less; His approval could not matter any more.

TIP #84

NO MATTER HOW MUCH EXPERIENCE YOU'VE HAD, REMAIN TEACHABLE.

Do You Know It All?

People who are know-it-alls suffer greatly, but the ones they hurt the most are themselves. Impressed with what they know, they miss out on what they don't know.

That is true of a know-it-all in every area, including evangelism. They've learned a lot about reaching the lost. Unfortunately, they've stopped learning more and become unteachable.

Proverbs 9:8–9 sets forth a basic principle, one that should be applied to many areas but most certainly to learning how to evangelize. We read,

Do not correct a scoffer, lest he hate you;
Rebuke a wise man, and he will love you.
Give instruction to a wise man, and he will be still wiser;
Teach a just man, and he will increase in learning.

One wastes time in trying to help a scoffer. He is too set against learning and becomes absolutely unteachable. A wise person, one who tries to walk with God, is a complete contrast. He knows a lot, but he is eager to learn more. That is why you can rebuke him or correct him and he receives it well. His hunger to learn drives his response. Give him any kind of biblical instruction you wish, and he will receive it gladly. He wants to know what he doesn't know. In one word, he's "teachable"—easy to correct, a delight to instruct.

The need for that teachability increases with age because the older we get, the more unteachable we tend to become.

What could anyone have to tell us when we've been around longer and have talked to more unbelievers than they have? Yes, increased experience can help us, but it can also hurt us. That is, we may be habitually doing something and fail to realize that it could and should be done better. While we don't want the meaning of our message to change, as time goes by, we may need to change how we say it. That may relate to everything from what we say, such as the terminology we use, to how we say it in terms of our demeanor.

The source of that instruction may be a friend, a book, a small group, a sermon, a failure, or a success in our own experience. But where the instruction comes from is not what makes the difference. The difference comes from how receptive we are to it.

What about you? Are you teachable or unteachable in evangelism?

TIP #85

FAITHFULNESS CAN PRESENT PROBLEMS, BUT IT CAN ALSO SOLVE PROBLEMS.

In and out of Trouble

Ever notice how something can have two sides to it, a negative and a positive? Oddly enough, it's the same way with faithfulness to God. It can get you in trouble. It can also get you out of trouble.

Consider Daniel in the Old Testament. He walked with God and was without fault. His enemies stated, "Then these men said, 'We shall not find any charge against this Daniel unless we find it against him concerning the law of his God'" (Daniel 6:5). So they instituted a plan and Daniel's faithfulness got him into trouble. They got King Darius to establish a law that whoever petitions any god or man for thirty days would be cast into the den of lions. When they caught Daniel praying, they told the king, "That Daniel, who is one of the captives from Judah, does not show due regard for you, O king, or for the decree that you have signed, but makes his petition three times a day" (Daniel 6:13).

But the faithfulness that got him into trouble also rescued him. When the king found Daniel alive in the lions' den, Daniel told him, "O king, live forever! My God sent His angel and shut the lions' mouths, so that they have not hurt me, because I was found innocent before Him; and also, O king, I have done no wrong before you" (Daniel 6:21–22).

Faithfulness in evangelism can cause you problems. Some might fault you for not saying something they deem more politically correct. Relatives might resent you bringing up the matter of their eternal salvation. A boss might be upset that you won't do something he requested that you knew was illegal or unethical. A friend may misrepresent what you told him.

But faithfulness can also rescue you. God hears the cries of those who walk closely to Him. Are we not told, "God is our refuge and strength, a very present help in trouble" (Psalm 46:1)? Those who obey Him in evangelism have seen Him do miracles in silencing the voices of accusers, establishing their innocence before others, and providing protection from physical harm (Psalm 138:8). They are on God's side but they also sense that He is on theirs.

Go ahead and be faithful in evangelism. It can get you into trouble, but it can also rescue you. God honors those who honor Him.

TIP #86

LEARN FROM YOUR EXPERIENCES; DON'T JUST PASS THROUGH THEM.

Your Best Teacher

We all have experiences. One followed by another. Some easy, some hard. Some excite us. Some exhaust us. The difference is some people learn from them, and others don't. To those who learn from them, experiences are some of the most valuable assets they can possess. Nothing can replace them. For those who don't learn from them, experiences are wasted. Instead of becoming experienced people, they are simply people who had experiences.

Examine Proverbs 10:14: "Wise people store up knowledge." Does that mean that wise people put knowledge in a container as one would place unused items in the basement or attic? Just the opposite. They gather it and store it so that it is available to them as they walk through life. The wise want to profit from what they've learned. It is like a well from which they draw daily.

Where does that knowledge come from? Proverbs would argue that much of it comes from life experiences. Examine a thought-provoking verse like Proverbs 19:20: "Listen to counsel and receive instruction, that you may be wise in your latter days." Note the phrase, "That you may be wise in your latter days." Experience takes time. Time brings experience. As you apply what you've learned, you become wiser and better at what you do.

Don't waste your evangelism experiences. After each person and each opportunity ask, "What did I learn? What can I do or not do next time?" Person by person, encounter by encounter, you build up tremendous wisdom in evangelism. The more you evangelize, the more you learn *how* to evangelize.

For example, you may have once hurried a conversation. You talked too much and listened too little. As a result you scared her off. She couldn't wait to escape you and the unpleasant conversation. Did that teach you something that will help in every conversation forthcoming? Take your time and listen.

Maybe another person once wanted to talk to you. The problem was you didn't want to talk to him. You were much more interested in reading the sports page of the newspaper. Your agenda became more important than his. What did you learn? Things of eternal significance are always more important than those which aren't.

"Christians are hypocrites." This is the tenth time you've heard it. What have you learned in terms of how to handle that objection? Learn what to say and that's one objection conquered. The more objections you hear and learn from, the more effective you are in evangelism.

Don't waste one of the most helpful commodities in evangelism—experiences. Each one makes you a spiritually wiser evangelist.

OVERCOME FEAR
IN EVANGELISM

TIP #87

FEAR IN EVANGELISM IS HELPFUL BECAUSE IT DRIVES YOU TO YOUR KNEES.

On Your Knees

One of the healthiest things in evangelism is fear. It sends us where evangelism needs to start—on our knees. There and then we recognize afresh our dependence on God.

Paul the apostle demonstrated this. He feared his own timidity and inadequacy so critically that not only did it send him to his knees, it drove others to their knees on his behalf. In Ephesians 6 he gave people one of his major prayer requests. He asked them to pray "that utterance may be given to me, that I may open my mouth boldly to make known the mystery of the gospel" (v. 19). Paul needed boldness and asked believers to pray for him.

Evangelism is characterized by two T's—tough and terrifying. Prayer gives us the strength to go on when we'd rather give up and the courage to speak when we'd rather clam up. That's what makes fear so healthy. On our knees, we recognize our dependence upon Him to give us what can only come from the Almighty's storage shed, an abundance of boldness for every situation where it's needed. Prayers for boldness have given many believers the courage in evangelism they never deemed possible. Being a prayer-answering God, He is quick to give us what we need. Many believers have testified that no sooner did they finish praying than they felt boldness that was not there moments earlier. Think about it: that boldness comes just for the asking!

Fear in evangelism can also cause us to pray more deeply for the lost. It's our praying for them, not just our pleading with them, that brings the lost to Christ. The people who have the most effective witness are the ones who spend a significant amount of time speaking to the lost about Christ and also speaking to Christ about the lost. Unless God works, unbelievers are not going to see their need, understand the simplicity of the gospel, or respond in faith. Prayer for them becomes not only a privilege but also a necessity.

When we let fear paralyze us, it is unhealthy, but when we let fear send us where we need to be anyway—on our knees—it shows us God's power in greater ways. As we sense our dependence upon Him to work on our behalf and on behalf of the non-Christian, we experience a burden for unbelievers and a boldness to talk to them.

TIP #88

TALK TO GOD WHILE YOU TALK TO THE OTHER PERSON.

God Hears the Whispers of the Heart

We know we should pray about evangelism, but did you know you can pray about evangelism while talking to an unbeliever? In the middle of our conversations with others, God is there, more real than the air you breathe, even though He is unseen, and we can carry on a conversation with God while having a conversation with an unbeliever.

God says in 1 Thessalonians 5:17, "Pray without ceasing." That doesn't mean to pray constantly because every moment cannot be given to prayer. It means to be consistent and persistent in prayer—praying at any moment at any place for anything. There is never a moment we can't pray if we wish. There is never anything we aren't free to pray about.

The reason is simple: *God hears the whispers of the heart.* I might be outwardly talking to you but at the same time inwardly speaking to God. The non-Christian hears me, but so does the God who cares more about the lost than I do. The unbeliever hears one conversation; God hears two: the one I'm having with the unbeliever and the one I'm having with Him. The faint whisper does not go unheard.

Why is that so helpful? Because as I engage in evangelism, help is always available—right now, right here. He is on call 24/7.

I may be speaking to an unbeliever and want to turn the conversation to spiritual things but can't figure out how to do so. From my heart, I cry out to God, "Help me and show me how." I may want to speak to a non-Christian about Christ, but I'm scared to death. My heart whispers, "God, give me boldness." When I've been insulted by a comment made by a non-Christian, my heart utters, "God, help me respond the way you would, not the way I want to." When I'm not sure how to answer a particular objection, I whisper, "God, help me know what to say." I may not want to take time out of a busy schedule to talk to an unbeliever, even though I should. My heart can cry out, "Help me now to rearrange my priorities."

Nowhere is the ability to talk to two people at the same time more beneficial than in evangelism. As you are attempting to bring someone into the kingdom, you can ask the assistance of the One who owns the kingdom. While talking to men, you can *always* whisper a prayer to God.

TIP #89

A PROPER FEAR OF GOD WILL DRIVE OUT YOUR FEAR OF MAN.

Helpful Fear

Fear is one of our greatest struggles in evangelism. Undoubtedly one of the biggest fears is the fear of rejection. That rejection may range from a friend who expresses disappointment that you would question his spiritual well-being to one who is outright angry and promises some type of retaliation.

How do you handle those difficult and fearful moments? The Scriptures offer several suggestions, but one is that it is important to know whom to fear.

Matthew 10:28 tells us, "And do not fear those who kill the body but cannot kill the soul. But rather fear Him who is able to destroy both soul and body in hell." Fear God, not man. The worst someone can do is kill the body. Should that happen to us as Christians, we are immediately in His presence. We are winners, not losers.

But God can do far more. He can sentence a person to eternal separation from God. Keep in mind that God will one day sentence the devil himself to a pit of fire and brimstone (Revelation 20:10).

Does that mean that we as Christians walk around physically shaken by the fact of what God might do to us? Certainly not. After all, once we trust Christ we are forever His children and nothing can separate us from Him. John 10:28 promises, "And I give them eternal life, and they shall never perish; neither shall anyone snatch them out of My hand."

The fear of God means that I stand in such awe of Him and His power that the thought of *not* speaking on His behalf and introducing others to Him is something I abhor. Many have called the fear of God "reverential trust." I so revere who He is and walk in such dependence on Him that I first and foremost want to please Him. No one in my life matters more or has more respect than He does. As I am consumed by that kind of fear, it has a healthy, positive impact upon my witness. What others might say or do doesn't matter. They may pass any sentence on me they wish, but the God I serve is so awesome He holds the power to sentence one to eternal separation from Him.

When a believer has a proper fear of God, there's no need to be controlled by an improper fear of others. What they might do is minuscule in comparison to what He is able to do.

Fear Him and there is no need to fear anyone or anything else.

TIP #90

A TRUE FRIEND TELLS PEOPLE WHAT THEY NEED TO HEAR, NOT NECESSARILY WHAT THEY WANT TO HEAR.

What Kind of Friend Are You?

Some friends are better than others. They tell you what you need to hear, not what you want to hear. A true friend focuses on you, not him. He cares more about you as a person than what he gets out of the friendship. Even though it could ultimately affect your relationship, he is you-centered, not self-centered.

This quality characterized Jesus and Peter's friendship. If ever there was a friend who told someone what he needed to hear, not just what he wanted to hear, it was Jesus. Jesus told Peter, "Assuredly, I say to you that this night, before the rooster crows, you will deny Me three times" (Matthew 26:34). Can you imagine how penetrating those words must have been to Peter? To think that his good friend, Jesus, would even entertain the thought that he, a disciple of His, would betray Him. Peter retorted, "Even if I have to die with You, I will not deny You!" (Matthew 26:35).

Hours later, Peter experienced the reality of what Christ had said. After denying Christ three times and immediately hearing the rooster crow, Peter remembered Christ's powerful words, "Before the rooster crows, you will deny Me three times" (v. 75). The verse continues, "So he went out and wept bitterly." What a friend Christ was to tell Peter what he needed to hear, not what he wanted to hear.

Suppose a believer enjoys speaking to others about Christ, but you are aware there is something about his life that is offensive to unbelievers. Do you hold back saying something to him because of the negative impact it could have on your friendship? Or do you tell him what he needs to hear, as Christ did Peter?

Now let's examine it from another angle. When we are indeed a friend to sinners as Christ was, we tell people the truth, regardless of what it means for our friendship. You know an unbeliever who needs to hear the gospel, but you are uncertain what saying something will mean to your relationship. The truth must always be expressed in grace, but it needs to be expressed. When we are concerned with losing the respect of a friend we should step back and check our motives. Is our major concern their relationship with us or their eternal relationship with the Lord?

What kind of friend are you to others?

TIP #91

CONSIDER WHAT UNBELIEVERS HAVE AHEAD OF THEM.

Yours versus Theirs

Believers know that they have no need to be ashamed of Christ. After all, why be ashamed to tell people about the One who took your place on a cross so that you could receive eternal life as a free gift? But that doesn't change the fact that the way unbelievers respond to you may make you *feel* ashamed. So how do you handle that feeling?

One answer is don't focus on *your* shame. Focus on *theirs*. Isaiah 44:11 tells us,

> Surely all his companions would be ashamed;
> and the workmen, they *are* mere men.
> Let them all be gathered together,
> let them stand up;
> yet they shall fear,
> they shall be ashamed together.

Isaiah is referring to those who are unbelievers. He specifically has in mind those who worship a false image instead of the one true God (vv. 9–10). When they see God face-to-face, what an absolutely horrible day it will be. Shame will be theirs as they see the One who has offered the eternal life that they've rejected. God will have no choice but to sentence them to eternal condemnation where they'll pay for their own sins. Recognizing how foolish they've been and the goodness of the God they rejected will be the most shame they've ever felt. Isaiah says, "And all shall be ashamed who are incensed against Him" (Isaiah 45:24). It's hard to even fathom to the fullest extent the shame and remorse that will be theirs.

With that in mind, compare the two shames. Yours is undeserved, theirs is deserved. Yours is feeling based; theirs is fact based. Yours is for doing what is necessary and right; theirs is for doing what's unnecessary and wrong. Yours is because of reverent living; theirs because of irreverent living. Worst of all, yours is temporary and theirs is eternal. Yours is escapable; theirs is inescapable.

The result? When considered in that light, it makes you grieve for them. You know what you face—a hope and a home for which you will never be ashamed. They have no idea what they are facing. Suddenly your concern is to share the gospel with them. How they make you feel becomes immaterial. It's your care and concern for them that make the difference. When looked at from that perspective, any shame *you* feel will quickly pass. *Their* shame will be there forever if they do not come to Christ.

TIP #92

ONE DIFFICULT NON-CHRISTIAN DOESN'T REPRESENT THEM ALL.

They're Not All Like That

A tactic that Satan likes to use with believers is the categorization of all unbelievers as the same. Count on it! I have seen it happen so many times.

Imagine that a believer decides he's going to be more consistent in his witness and grasp every opportunity available. Along comes the first person. Wouldn't you know it? That particular non-Christian turns out to be one of the hardest, most disinterested people toward the gospel any believer could ever meet.

That's when Satan walks in. Immediately he convinces the believer, "That's what they're all like. Go ahead if you want, but you are wasting your time."

Of course, Satan hopes you never find out what Jesus Christ, in truth, called him: a liar, and the father of lies. In John 8, Jesus rebukes the Pharisees—Israel's spiritual leaders—for believing Satan's lies that Christ was not who He claimed to be. Jesus said,

> "You are of your father the devil, and the desires of your father you want to do. He was a murderer from the beginning, and does not stand in the truth, because there is no truth in him. When he speaks a lie, he speaks from his own resources, for he is a liar and the father of it." (John 8:44)

Because they believed Satan, the Pharisees kept many from following Christ. Satan's specialty is always lies, not truth.

Committed to lying, Satan doesn't have just one lie he'll use. He has a bottomless bucket of them. He pulls the one from that bucket of lies that he hopes you will accept. He wants you to believe that one negative conversation represents them all. But the next non-Christian you encounter may be the one who is so ready for the gospel he is like fruit about to fall off a branch. Keep going and you may be surprised how many approachable people you find.

If Satan told you the truth, he would tell you what evangelists and anyone consistent in evangelism discovers. Yes, there are those who are completely closed to the gospel. In no uncertain terms, they make it clear that they have no desire to discuss spiritual things. But they are the exception, not the norm. In almost every community, those who are willing to discuss spiritual matters when they are properly approached outnumber those who are not. Besides, God honors consistent obedience. Those who keep evangelizing have the joy of walking through God-opened doors.

So when you meet the closed person, respond to Satan by saying, "So what? They're not all like that."

TIP #93

UNDERSTANDING THE CAUSE BEHIND THE REJECTION MAKES IT EASIER TO BEAR.

Rejection Hurts

Rejection is no fun. As a knife cuts to the bone, rejection cuts deep. It makes us feel worthless. In simple terms, it can suck the life out of our witness.

Paul the apostle understood rejection. It was one of the many afflictions he suffered in ministry. He spoke of these afflictions when he said, "We are hard-pressed on every side, yet not crushed; we are perplexed, but not in despair; persecuted, but not forsaken; struck down, but not destroyed" (2 Corinthians 4:8–9). "Hard-pressed" carries the idea that what came at him came from every side, every direction he turned. There were times that every place he turned he felt like he was surrounded by the enemy. "Perplexed" conveys that he felt at a loss of what to do. He was at the same point we are when we say, "Now what do I do?" But note the combination of words: *Hard-pressed . . . yet not crushed. Perplexed . . . but not in despair; persecuted, but not forsaken; struck down, but not destroyed.* His emotions could have made it hard to carry on, but his mind told him the situation wasn't hopeless.

So what did he do? What kept him evangelizing? Two things:

One, he reminded himself that lost people are blinded. Until the Holy Spirit works they will never see or understand their need for Christ. He says in verses 3–4, "But even if our gospel is veiled, it is veiled to those who are perishing, whose minds the god of this age has blinded."

Second, he reminded himself that the source of the gospel's power was from above not from within. He says, "But we have this treasure in earthen vessels, that the excellence of the power may be of God and not of us" (2 Corinthians 4:7). We must depend on Him to work through us. The power to evangelize and the power that brings people to Christ is of God.

Only after Paul writes about these two truths can he talk about his rejection without dejection. Clinging to this knowledge allows Paul to combine persecution with hope.

So when rejection hits, remind yourself: Only God can dispel blindness. Only God's power working in us and through us can bring them to Christ. Will that relieve the agony of the rejection? Probably not. We may still experience pain and hurt. Rejection is never a pleasant experience. But it will cause us to respond properly. Although feeling at a loss of what to do, we can endure. We can look up, then speak up, not give up.

IMPACT YOUR CHURCH
IN EVANGELISM

TIP #94

YOU PLAY A VITAL ROLE IN YOUR CHURCH'S REPUTATION.

Don't Minimize Its Importance

It can take just one Sunday to split a church, but it can take as long as five years to recover from it. Most unfortunate of all is the way it can impact the witness you as a Christian have to the lost. How many times have you heard unbelievers say, "Why should I come to Christ when even the Christians cannot get along with each other?" Christians often realize that conflict within their assembly can deeply hurt their relationships with one another. Sadly, they often overlook the even greater damage it has done in their relationships with unbelievers outside the church.

Through your involvement in a local church, you play a vital role in your church's reputation. When Paul wrote to the church in Ephesus, he was addressing every member of it. He said to them in Ephesians 4:3, "endeavoring to keep the unity of the Spirit in the bond of peace." Paul wanted them to know that unity did not come naturally; it was something that they had to work hard to keep.

One verse prior he addressed the kind of spirit that leads to unity. He told them, "with all lowliness and gentleness, with long-suffering, bearing with one another in love." A simple look at those words tells us what qualities need to characterize us if we are going to contribute to the unity of the church. We should have a gentle and humble attitude in our relationships with one another. Just as we ask God to be patient with us, we should be patient with our brothers and sisters in Christ. When others wrong us we should be long-suffering, accepting injury without fighting back. We should bear *with* one another, not *be* a bear with one another!

Two questions. Are you a help or hindrance when it comes to contributing to the unity of your church? What concrete steps are you taking to enhance unity and even encourage others to do the same? All kinds of ideas should come to mind—resolving conflicts face-to-face now instead of later, forgetting and forgiving instead of forgetting to forgive, concentrating on other people's strengths not their faults, praising one another before the assembly, and putting other people's needs before yours.

But heavy on your mind should be the "why"—the non-Christians in your community. To enhance your witness to the lost, help make your church's reputation a good one.

TIP #95

HELP YOUR CHURCH BE WHAT IT SHOULD BE INSTEAD OF COMPLAINING ABOUT WHAT IT ISN'T.

Run with It

Many concerned about the lost become frustrated with those who, from their observation, aren't. As they think of their own church's evangelism program, they see little if anything happening. They often become critical of both leadership and laypeople. "Our church has no heart for the lost," they say, or, "We aren't doing anything to reach our community. We don't even have an evangelism training program."

Two things often result. First, that attitude can cause more harm than good as Satan uses it to divide and damage. Second, that negative attitude rarely does anything but hurt.

Biblically, we should not be a drawback to our church's evangelism program; we should be what is referred to in the world of football as a fullback. A drawback pulls the church back. A fullback takes the ball and runs with it.

Hebrews 10:24–25 teaches us what our attitude should be toward the local church:

And let us consider one another in order to stir up love and good works, not forsaking the assembling of ourselves together, as is the manner of some, but exhorting one another, and so much the more as you see the Day approaching.

"To stir up" has the idea of provoking one another. But notice the emphasis is provoking "love and good works." Simply put, the writer of Hebrews is saying, be a fullback, not a drawback.

As it relates to your church's evangelism program, start with prayer—prayer for the leadership, prayer for the lay-people, and prayer for yourself. Then ask God, "What would you have me do?" Why not share your concern with the leadership? Perhaps they are as burdened as you are, and together you can figure out what needs to be done. Why not lead a church evangelism-training program using the abundance of training materials available? Is there an event coming up that could be used to reach the lost? What might you do to make that one of the most effective outreaches the church has had?

Approach the situation with a God-honoring attitude and watch what happens. Before long, others may be speaking of the church's evangelism program's impact upon non-Christians, recognizing how drastically the situation has improved. Because God used you to be a fullback, not a drawback, they may be saying, "Our church has never been evangelistic, but it is now."

TIP #96

BEING AN EXAMPLE IS ESSENTIAL TO ENCOURAGING OTHERS IN EVANGELISM.

Motivating Others

An illustration is worth a thousand words. When you tell someone something, they often respond, "I hear it." When you illustrate it, they respond, "I see it."

An illustration does not only help us understand. When that illustration becomes a living flesh example, it also motivates us. Often church leaders exhort us to talk to our relatives and friends about Christ, but only some leaders stand out—those who share their compassion for the lost through their own examples of speaking to unbelievers about the Savior. In other words, the ones who illustrate it with their own lives. Their example captivates you, and their excitement spreads. You think of your own missed opportunities and somehow you leave their presence wanting to be more like them in talking to the lost. They excite you by what they did, even more than by what they said. Example does more than exhortation.

Leading by example is a biblical approach. As Paul discipled Christians in the Corinthian church, he said, "Imitate me, just as I also imitate Christ" (1 Corinthians 11:1). Motivated by a desire to help others, he led by example and encouraged the Corinthians to follow his model.

Paul and Peter together also taught church leaders to lead by example. Paul said to Timothy, his son in the faith, "But you be watchful in all things, endure affliction, do the work of an evangelist, fulfill your ministry" (2 Timothy 4:5). Timothy was instructed to *do* the work of an evangelist, not just talk about it. Peter told church leaders, "Shepherd the flock of God which is among you, serving as overseers, not by compulsion but willingly, not for dishonest gain but eagerly; nor as being lords over those entrusted to you, but being examples to the flock" (1 Peter 5:2–3). Note that Peter taught the church leaders to be and do what they were asking their people to be and do. This would most certainly include evangelism. Peter understood the need to lead by practicing, not just by preaching.

If you want others to evangelize, remember the simple principle that example does more than exhortation. All of us are captivated by those who not only tell others what to do, but do it themselves. Even if they cannot observe you in an actual situation, if they know you are actually doing it, it motivates them.

Want others to evangelize? Lead by example so that they will not only hear what you say, but also see what you do.

TIP #97

MULTIPLY YOUR WITNESS BY TRAINING OTHERS AS WELL.

Increase Your Impact

Take the number two and add two to it ten times. The equation's answer is so simple that you don't need a calculator. The total is twenty-two. Now take the same number two and multiply it by two, ten times. You *will* need a calculator. The answer is 2048. The difference is phenomenal.

Translate that into evangelism. Suppose you train one other person in how to evangelize, sharing with him what the Lord has taught you. Now those two people know how to present the gospel to the lost. Then suppose that each one of you train another and that process happens ten times over. Instead of two people attempting to evangelize their world, you now have 2048 sharing the gospel. Multiplying yourself works.

Not one of us can take credit for this strategy. Before we were even alive, Christ taught His followers to mimic what He taught. It's stated in ten simple words: "Follow Me, and I will make you fishers of men" (Matthew 4:19). Those original disciples eventually resulted in the local church. Paul followed Christ's pattern when he trained young Timothy and told him to train others. Second Timothy 2:2 says, "And the things you have heard from me among many witnesses, commit these to faithful men who will be able to teach others also."

If you are consistent in evangelism, you will have tremendous opportunities to share the gospel. Some of those you speak to will trust the Savior at that moment. Others may come to Christ months or even years later. For those who don't receive His free gift, you've nonetheless been faithful in spreading the good news. Don't limit the impact of your life. Let it spill over onto others you can train. Think of how exciting it would be to hear of opportunities they have had that you will never have. They work around people you will never meet, so they become an extension of your voice. You witnessed to those unbelievers, but you did it through the person you trained.

Challenge them then not to limit the impact of their lives either. After they are trained, encourage them to train someone else. Impart to them the vision of how their witness can be extended through the multiplication of themselves.

The outcome will be that more people will hear the gospel than you could ever have approached yourself. All because by following Christ's example, your life was committed to multiplication. Teaching those who can teach others has phenomenal results.

HELP NEW CHRISTIANS GROW

TIP #98

TELL NEW CHRISTIANS WHERE TO START IN THEIR STUDY OF THE WORD.

Inadequate Instructions

My friends who taught me how to water-ski gave me inadequate instructions. They forgot to tell me what to do when I lost my balance and fell down. I had to figure it out on my first attempt after swallowing half the lake: let go of the rope! A simple but overlooked instruction.

We make the same mistake with new converts who want to grow as Christians. We sometimes give inadequate instructions. We say to them, "Now since you are a Christian, read the Bible." We even tell them why. We explain, "God wants to feed you spiritually." In one way or another we share with them the truth of 2 Timothy 3:16–17: "All Scripture is given by inspiration of God, and is profitable for doctrine, for reproof, for correction, for instruction in righteousness, that the man of God may be complete, thoroughly equipped for every good work." The problem is we don't tell them where to start. They may not even realize that the Bible consists of sixty-six books written independently of each other.

Not knowing any differently, new Christians often start with Genesis. Quickly, they get lost in the genealogies of chapter five. They come away saying, "I just don't understand the Bible."

Start on an infancy level. Paul said, "But we were gentle among you, just as a nursing *mother* cherishes her own children" (1 Thessalonians 2:7). Then he continued, "as you know how we exhorted, and comforted, and charged every one of you, as a father *does* his own children" (v. 11). An easy book for a new Christian to begin with is Philippians. It talks about daily Christian living right there where feet and street meet. The new believer will learn about suffering, humility, selfishness, sharing, complaining, rejoicing, spiritual growth, prayer, anxiety, the mind, and even Christian giving. In short, they'll be dining at the smorgasbord of God.

It helps to tell them to take a chapter a day and pick one truth to meditate upon that day. Encourage them to stay in Philippians for a month. Since it has four chapters, at the pace of one chapter a day, they will have read the book seven times. They'll see things each time they overlooked in the previous reading.

Don't give inadequate instructions to a new convert. New believers need to know not merely what to read, but where to read. Invite them to dine at the Word of God, but be careful to tell them which dish to sample first.

TIP #99

DON'T CONFUSE SALVATION AND DISCIPLESHIP.

A Helpful Clarification

Confusing what is free with what is costly can be dangerous and detrimental. My wife and I once received an invitation to a free vacation in the mountains. If we didn't understand it was free, we could've missed out on a refreshing few days in the outdoors. Had it not actually been free, though, it could've cost us money we were not prepared to spend. Clarity was essential.

Nowhere is there more danger in confusing what is free with what is not than in the area of salvation and discipleship.

Our salvation, God's offer of eternal life, is completely free for us with no strings attached. Revelation 22:17 says, "And the Spirit and the bride say, 'Come!' And let him who hears say, 'Come!' And let him who thirsts come. Whoever desires, let him take the water of life freely." In this verse, "water of life" is a metaphor for eternal life. Eternal life is free to us because Christ took the punishment we deserved and rose again. The price having been paid, God can now extend eternal life free.

At the same time, discipleship costs. A disciple is a learner, someone who follows after Christ and learns more about Him. Christ was quick to encourage those who wanted to be His disciples to consider the cost before enlisting. Christ specifically stated the cost in Luke 14:26–27:

> If anyone comes to Me and does not hate his father and mother, wife and children, brothers and sisters, yes, and his own life also, he cannot be My disciple. And whoever does not bear his cross and come after Me cannot be My disciple.

The costs are threefold: loyalty to Christ must have priority over any earthly ties, Jesus Christ must have the ownership of our lives, and we must be willing to suffer humiliation, hardship, and even death for His sake. For those willing to bear that cost, there is great reward. Christ promised, "And behold, I am coming quickly, and My reward is with Me, to give to everyone according to his work" (Revelation 22:12).

A failure to see that salvation is free could cause one to depend on his own efforts to save him and thus be separated from God forever. A failure to see the cost of discipleship can cause one to consider too lightly what it means to follow after Him.

Salvation and discipleship, one free, the other costly. Don't confuse the two. The first cost Christ His life, the second may cost you yours.

TIP #100

PATIENCE AND TENDER LOVING CARE CAN HELP GET NEW BELIEVERS EXCITED ABOUT CHURCH.

Church and the New Christian

To many non-Christians, God is attractive; church is not. God might be attractive for many reasons. There is something about His love that is beyond anything the secular world has ever experienced. They've seen Him turn a friend's life inside out. Instead of contemplating suicide, their friend is excited to be alive. They've heard some pretty awesome stories followed by, "Just think what God could do in your life."

Still, church may not be attractive. The building is intimidating to look at and much more intimidating to enter. People seem rather cold and unfriendly. The services can be boring and long, filled with unfamiliar songs and an unrelateable message. The speaker's specialty can seem to be guilt trips. Hence, a person who comes to Christ this week may not necessarily be in church next week.

That's why new converts need an abundance of TLC—the tender, loving care that could cause them to progress from having made a decision for Christ to becoming a disciple of Christ.

No one appeared to understand that better than Paul the apostle. Two verses spell out what could be called his follow-up strategy. In 1 Thessalonians 2:7, he wrote "But we were gentle among you, just as a nursing mother cherishes her own children." What could drive home a more caring, patient, loving, tender-hearted spirit than the image of a nursing mother caring for her baby? The child at this point isn't fully aware of his own needs, but the gentle spirit of the mother helps him grow.

Then Paul draws an analogy from the masculine side. He says in 1 Thessalonians 2:11, "as you know how we exhorted, and comforted, and charged every one of you, as a father does his own children." The idea is, "I did whatever I had to do in laying out the path for you to walk and helped you to walk it." A caring father doesn't say, "There's the path. Lots of luck. Go for it." A caring father says, "Here's where to go and how to live. Let's walk it together."

That kind of TLC draws people close to you, a step that precedes drawing them close to your church. Eventually with your encouragement and your example to follow after Christ as His disciple, they will most likely come to church. Patience and tender care will help a new convert who's excited about Christ to get excited about church.

TIP #101

AS YOU GIVE ASSURANCE OF SALVATION TO A CHILD, EMPHASIZE A FACT, NOT A DATE.

How to Help a Child

Caring parents want to do all they can to nurture their children, but sometimes unintentionally, especially in the spiritual realm, they hinder instead of help.

As a child grows and begins to understand the gospel better, he can wonder if he's really saved. The parents, wanting to assure the child, might tell him they remember the day he asked Jesus into his heart. But the child doesn't remember the event as well as his parents do. Besides, what if the child didn't truly understand the gospel and trust Christ? The mouthing of a prayer has never saved anyone.

Interestingly enough, when Scripture gives assurance of salvation, it doesn't go back to a date or a place. It goes back to a fact. That is, what is one trusting in right now for eternal life? If a person is trusting Christ alone to save him, he's saved regardless of when and where that happened. True, there is a split second when one crosses from darkness into light, but whether or not we know the date has nothing to do with assurance of salvation.

So upon interacting with a child about his salvation, one should ask him, "What are you trusting in right now as your only way to heaven?" If the child is trusting Christ alone, knowing He paid the debt in his place, he is right now and forever a child of God. When or where he "crossed the line" into salvation is not the issue.

Take a child to the verse he may know the best, John 3:16: "For God so loved the world that He gave His only begotten Son, that whoever believes in Him should not perish but have everlasting life." Note that it says, "Whoever believes in Him should not perish." It does not say, "Whoever believes in Him and *knows the date* that their belief began." Assurance is based on the fact that we have trusted Christ—period.

Imagine how freeing that is to a child (or an adult, for that matter). As he grows and understands the depth of God's love better, he need not be concerned with *when* he became a child of God. He can relax in the fact that whenever and wherever he trusted Christ, he became and remains forever His child.

Interact with the child in such a way that he knows if he's saved and he knows why. Not only will you help your children, you may also help them know how to help their children.

ABOUT THE AUTHOR

Dr. Larry Moyer, Founder and CEO of EvanTell, is a frequent speaker in evangelistic outreaches, training seminars, churches, and classrooms across the world. He is a regular guest lecturer in evangelism at Word of Life Bible Institutes in New York and Florida and visiting professor at Dallas Theological Seminary, and has earned degrees from Cairn University (BS), Dallas Theological Seminary (ThM), and Gordon-Conwell Seminary (DMin). In 2001, Cairn University also awarded him the honorary Doctor of Sacred Theology degree. He is contributing editor of *The Evangelism Study Bible*, and has many other books, including:

21 Things God Never Said: Correcting Our Misconceptions about Evangelism

31 Days with the Master Fisherman: A Daily Devotional for Bringing Christ to Others

31 Days to Contagious Living

31 Days Walking with God in the Workplace

31 Days to Growing as a New Believer

Free and Clear: Understanding and Communicating God's Offer of Eternal Life

Show Me How to Share the Gospel

Show Me How to Answer Tough Questions

Show Me How To Share Christ in the Workplace

Show Me How to Develop Evangelistic Sermons

Show Me How to Illustrate Evangelistic Messages

ABOUT EVANTELL

EvanTell is an international evangelism ministry headquartered in Dallas, TX. Founded by Dr. R. Larry Moyer in 1973, its mission is to declare the gospel clearly and simply, activate believers around the world, and prepare upcoming generations to reach the world. Since its inception, it has presented the gospel to more than 32 million people and presently facilitates fifty thousand evangelism trainings each year. Its materials are available in fifty-nine languages worldwide, reaching and equipping others in evangelism. The ministry serves churches, academic institutions, parachurch organizations, pregnancy resource centers, mission organizations, and individuals.